MOTABILITY

MOTABILITY
The Road to Freedom

Allan Beard

The Book Guild Ltd
Sussex, England

The Book Guild Ltd
25 High Street,
Lewes, Sussex

First published 1998
© Allan Beard 1998

Set in Times
Typesetting by
Acorn Bookwork, Salisbury, Wiltshire

Printed in Great Britain by
Bookcraft (Bath) Ltd, Avon

A catalogue record for this book is
available from the British Library

ISBN 1 85776 397 1

For Helen

CONTENTS

viii

PATRONS, OFFICERS AND MEMBERS

Chief Patron – Her Majesty the Queen

Patrons

The Rt Hon Paddy Ashdown MP
The Rt Hon Tony Blair MP
The Rt Hon Baroness Chalker
The Rt Hon William Hague MP
The Rt Hon Harriet Harman MP
Baroness Hollis
Glenda Jackson MP
The Rt Hon Lord Jenkin
The Rt Hon Peter Lilley MP
The Rt Hon John Major MP
The Rt Hon Lord Morris of Manchester AO QSO
The Rt Hon Lord Newton OBE
The Rt Hon Andrew Smith MP
The Rt Hon Baroness Thatcher LG OM FRS

Life Vice-Presidents

Lord Attenborough CBE
Lord Rayne
Sir Evelyn de Rothschild
Roly Stafford OBE

Governors

Chairman: The Rt Hon The Lord Sterling of Plaistow CBE
Vice Chairman: Gerald Acher
Hon. Treasurer: Sir John Quinton

ix

FOREWORD

It is amazing to think that 21 years have passed since Motability was created. It seems only yesterday that Lord Goodman and I discussed its inception with Allan Beard who was the Under Secretary deputed by the then Secretary of State, the late Lord Ennals, and Permanent Secretary, Sir Patrick Nairne, to represent the Department of Health and Social Security. Indeed it was Allan Beard who dreamed up the name 'Motability'.

Arnold Goodman considered Motability, which enjoys all-party support, to be a unique partnership between Government and the private sector. I think it is most appropriate that Allan Beard has set out here not only to record the organisation's history but also to explain its present-day workings. More importantly, he records and thanks the very large number of 'unsung heroes' who have played so vital a part in the organisation's success.

All of us who have been involved during the past 21 years have gained a great deal of pleasure and satisfaction from working together with the common goal of providing a 'Road to Freedom' for disabled people. Motability has been our way of putting something back into society.

The Rt Hon The Lord Sterling of Plaistow CBE

INTRODUCTION

My thanks are due to all those who have helped me to compile
this account of Motability and its history. They include my
fellow Governors, the staff of Motability and civil servants
from the Government Departments concerned. I particularly
wish to acknowledge the help given by the late Lord Ennals,
Lord Morris, Sir Patrick Nairne and Lord Sterling in agreeing
to be interviewed about their recollection of the events leading
to the setting-up of Motability.

I am indebted to Gerry Acher for advice and help, and to
the late Alan Outten, for many years a Governor of
Motability, for help with Chapter 4, dealing with Motability
Finance Limited (MFL). Sir John Quinton and the Chief
Executive of MFL, Ed Lester, have also assisted me with
this chapter. As is explained in the text, I have made use
of the survey reports written by the late Professor Gerald
Hoinville and Dr Wendy Sykes, and by Tracy Savill and
Richard Stait.

At the same time I must make it clear that I alone am
responsible for the contents of this work, and its accuracy. The
account represents my own views, which should not necessarily
be taken to be accepted by the people mentioned above. In
particular, it in no way commits Motability or the Government
Departments concerned.

In general the history records events up to the end of
1997, although necessarily many of the statistics are of an
earlier date. This seemed to be a good time to which to take
the story of the establishment of the charity and its subsequent
development, because of the great expansion that has been
taking place recently in the demands made upon it and the

many changes now under way to keep pace with this growth. Inevitably, because of the rapid rate of those changes, not all of them can be fully dealt with here, but I have wherever possible dealt with significant changes in progress. My object has been not only to record the history of Motability but also to give a full account of the way in which its schemes work.

Although I have tried to bring out the part so many people have played in the story of Motability, I think it is right to single out for mention here the initiative taken by Lord Ennals and Lord Morris in 1977, and the essential part played in the creation and later development of the charity by Lord Goodman and Lord Sterling.

Barry James and Ken Keen, who built up Motability as Directors; Robin Taylor, for so many years its Assistant Director; and the hardworking and dedicated staff of Motability must also be mentioned. I would in addition especially pay tribute to Gerry Acher, who has contributed so much, both before and after taking over my position in the governance of the charity; and to the new Director, Noel Muddiman, who has so rapidly improved Motability's organisation and management since his appointment in 1995.

MFL and its staff have of course made a valuable and essential contribution to the success of the Motability Scheme.

The part played by the disabled Governors, Sir Peter Large, Joe Hennessy and Adrian Stokes, and by George Wilson, Alan Outten and Roly Stafford, all of whom have given generously of their time over the years, has been of great importance.

Special reference should also be made to the support and encouragement received over many years from Departmental Ministers and their permanent secretaries and staff, in particular from a former Minister for Disabled People, the Rt Hon Sir Nicholas Scott KBE, who was a true friend of Motability.

I am grateful to Motability for agreeing to meet the cost of publishing my book. I would also like to thank my publishers, the Book Guild, for their help and encouragement.

Above all, I would like to thank my wife, without whose

patience and forbearance it would not have been possible for me to compile the story of Motability.

Allan Beard

Note: For convenience I have normally used the single word 'Department' throughout the text to mean the Department of Health and Social Security and its successors, the Department of Social Security and the Department of Health. This reference also includes the Scottish Office, the Welsh Office and the Northern Ireland Office where appropriate.

1

HOW MOTABILITY STARTED

Motability is an organisation which has changed the lives of hundreds of thousands of disabled people. They are severely disabled persons who are unable, or virtually unable, to walk – those with cerebral palsy, spina bifida, muscular atrophy and many other conditions. They are of all ages, including children from the age of five upwards.

Their lives have been changed because, being unable to afford a car or powered wheelchair from their own resources, they have been able to have one through the Motability Scheme. No longer housebound, they can go out with their families for social visits, holidays, shopping, visits to the doctor or hospital, and for many other purposes, either as drivers or as passengers.

These changes have been brought about by a unique organisation in which the Department of Social Security, the clearing banks, motor manufacturers and dealers, insurance companies, motoring associations and voluntary effort have come together with a common purpose. They were able to do so because of an important change which the Government made in 1976 in its provision for the mobility of severely disabled people – the introduction of a universal cash mobility allowance in place of a limited 'vehicle scheme' for drivers only. It is the combination of the mobility allowance and Motability which made possible the great changes which are described in this history.

1

THE OLD GOVERNMENT VEHICLE SCHEME

The Government vehicle scheme, which in its final form had been in operation since 1948, was for people virtually unable to walk, provided that they could drive, although a particular group were admitted who were slightly less disabled but who needed transport to get to work or because of domestic responsibilities. About one-third of all beneficiaries were in this latter category. the Scheme provided on permanent loan a single-seater invalid three-wheeler – the 'trike' – maintained and insured free of charge, exempt from vehicle excise duty (the road fund licence), and with a £10 a year allowance towards petrol tax.

Alternatively, from 1972 the Government provided a private car allowance (the PCA) for those among the same group of disabled people who wished to drive their own car – £100 a year tax-free, plus exemption from vehicle excise duty. A restricted group of people – e.g. women with young children whom they could not leave on their own – could have a small car instead of the trike, with the same accompanying benefits, except that there was an allowance towards maintenance of the car instead of free maintenance.

For a period from 1963 onwards there was another alternative to the trike – a grant of £90 every five years for the installation of hand controls to the disabled person's own car.

At 31 March 1976 the numbers of people in the UK benefiting from the Scheme were:

Trikes	21,191
Cars	4,939
PCA	23,437
	49,567

It was significant that more people chose the PCA than the trike – i.e. they could afford to obtain or already had a car and could manage to run it with the aid of the PCA. This trend was even more striking in new cases – in the closing years of the Scheme, 1974 to 1976, nearly twice as many people chose the PCA as the trike. Eventually, however, the replacement of their car no doubt posed a problem for some of them.

Advantages and disadvantages of the trike

Although, as we shall see, the trike had its faults, it had given good service over the years. It is of interest to note that its origins go back to the provision by the Government in 1922 of motorised bathchairs for disabled servicemen of the First World War. These vehicles were improved over the years and became available to civilian disabled people with the commencement of the National Health Service in 1948. The trike, for all its limitations, was a cleverly designed vehicle, with, in its final stages, a fibreglass body, sliding doors, automatic transmission and a variety of methods of steering. Electric propulsion was also available. A tribute should be paid to the engineers of the Department and the manufacturers who developed it to the limit of its capabilities and who devised many special adaptations to meet particular needs.

There is no doubt that many trike drivers looked on their vehicles with great affection. But the trike had shortcomings, which had long been recognised. It did not have a good safety record, particularly in the hands of young drivers. Given the inherently less stable characteristics of a three-wheeler as compared with a conventional car, it was not practicable to redesign it to keep pace with general road vehicle developments and to meet the increasingly stringent demands of European Union and national safety regulations. Moreover, a trike driver was not allowed to carry passengers, so that wives, husbands, family and friends had to be left behind – the trike was not a 'sociable' vehicle.

PRESSURE FOR CHANGE

Government cars had been available for 100 per cent disabled war pensioners since 1948, both as drivers and as passengers, and this provision was later extended to those with lower rates of disability. The Invalid Tricycle Association (which became the Disabled Drivers Association in 1963) and the Joint Committee on Mobility for Disabled People (JCMD) pressed the Government strongly for the same provision for civilians.

In the early 1960s it was the JCMD – comprising the representatives of some 22 national disability organisations and a number of individual experts – which first began to press the case of disabled passengers for personal transport, calling the exclusion of these severely disabled people 'a cruel anomaly', and describing it as illogical nonsense 'to base a service for the physically disabled on a physical ability – the ability to drive'.

In 1968 the JCMD submitted a statement of its case to Mr David (later Lord) Ennals, then Minister of State at the newly reorganised Department of Health and Social Security. It asked for parity of treatment between disabled drivers and disabled passengers, and a choice of a mobility grant or an issued car as an alternative to the trike. It opposed the abolition of the trike, claiming that it was a welcome means of mobility for many disabled drivers. The JCMD's representations, backed up by case histories, were resubmitted to the Department in 1970.

In 1971 a mass protest rally was held by the Disabled Drivers Association in Trafalgar Square, pressing for a choice for disabled people between the trike and a car, and this was followed by a meeting with the Prime Minister.

A strong campaign for the abolition of the trike on safety grounds was mounted by the Disabled Drivers Action Group, formed in 1973, and later by the Invalid Tricycle Action Group, supported by the racing driver, Graham Hill. This was accompanied by a great deal of newspaper and parliamentary pressure about the trike.

BARONESS SHARP'S REVIEW

Because of this growing criticism from many quarters of the lack of comprehensive provision for mobility, the Secretary of

State for Social Services, Sir Keith (later Lord) Joseph, announced in 1972 the introduction of the PCA as a means of reducing dependence on the trike, and also the setting up of a major review of the vehicle scheme by Baroness Sharp. Following widespread consultation, the JCMD made a submission to Baroness Sharp on the same lines as the representations to the Minister of State in 1968.

Baroness Sharp's terms of reference had required her to make proposals within the limits of available resources. In her report, published in March 1974, she therefore felt obliged to recommend that the benefits she proposed should be available only to those severely disabled people who were in employment, education or training. Her proposal was that the trike should be phased out over a period of four to five years and replaced by a small car. Disabled non-drivers would be eligible on the same terms as disabled drivers.

Following the publication of the report, the JCMD once again expressed its opposition to the abolition of the trike and demanded a mobility grant scheme as the basic solution. Baroness Sharp's proposals were in fact condemned by virtually all interested groups, most of whom now agreed with the JCMD's proposals for a mobility grant scheme.

The Scheme proposed by Baroness Sharp was not adopted by Lord Joseph or the succeeding Secretary of State, Mrs Barbara (now Baroness) Castle, because, although the position of existing beneficiaries would no doubt have been protected, the prospect of mobility would have been taken away from the great majority of people who would have qualified under the old scheme – i.e. those too severely disabled to work.

THE END OF THE VEHICLE SCHEME

Baroness Castle was succeeded by Lord Ennals, who, together with Lord Morris, the author of the Chronically Sick and Disabled Persons Act, 1970, and the Minister for Disabled People, decided to make a radical change in mobility provision for severely disabled people. In 1976 the vehicle scheme was abolished for new entrants, and a completely new system – the mobility allowance – took its place. In other words, the Government decided to replace hardware with cash. Although the new scheme would undoubtedly cost more, it would have the advantage ultimately of doing away with the administratively expensive system of direct provision and maintenance of the trike.

The vehicle scheme was continued for existing beneficiaries, and the £10 a year petrol allowance was increased to £40 in 1991. Existing trike drivers were told that the Government expected to be able to keep them provided with a trike suitable to their requirements, if they still wished to have one, until at least 1982 or 1983, and probably for much longer. They were also promised that if their increased disability made a trike unsuitable, efforts would be made to provide them with a car which they could drive. These promises have been fulfilled: there are still some 1,000 trikes in use by those who wish to keep them, and Government funds have been made available to enable trike drivers to enter the Motability contract hire scheme (see Chapter 5).

THE NEW MOBILITY ALLOWANCE

The introduction of the mobility allowance took account of the most important defect of the old scheme – even more important than the shortcomings of the trike – which was that it gave help only to those who could drive, and none whatsoever to those who were just as much in need of mobility but could only be passengers because they were too badly disabled to drive or were below driving age.

The basic philosophy was that a benefit in the form of cash enabled recipients to choose the method of achieving mobility which suited them best – e.g. driving a car, being driven by relatives or friends, or taking a taxi or hired car. For those who chose to have a car, there was the added benefit of being able to choose the most suitable type of vehicle and model.

The new scheme, starting on 1 January 1976, provided cash

help with mobility at the rate of £4 a week for all those between age 5 and pensionable age who had a disability severely affecting mobility – i.e. who were virtually unable to walk, whether or not they were capable of driving or old enough to drive.

The Government's stated aim was to increase the rate of the allowance in real terms when resources were available – a promise which was later fulfilled, and, as explained in the next chapter, made the Motability Scheme possible. The allowance was at first taxable, on the basis that this ensured that the greatest help went to those in the greatest need. Liability to tax was, however, removed in 1982.

The original upper age limit of pensionable age (65 for men and 60 for women) for the first award of the allowance was raised to 65 for women in 1979. People qualifying before 65 could continue to receive the allowance, originally for ten years, later to age 80, and from 1992 onwards indefinitely.

It was originally estimated that 150,000 people would qualify for the mobility allowance, but the number grew steadily over the years and is now well over 1,500,000.

Beneficiaries under the old vehicle scheme were entitled to transfer to the mobility allowance without a medical examination, and they were given reserved rights to receive the allowance for life.

LIMITATIONS OF THE MOBILITY ALLOWANCE

Several motor manufacturers offered a special discount to disabled people. Furthermore, for hire purchase of cars by disabled people the Government relaxed the control orders governing the minimum deposit and the maximum period of repayment. It was clear, however, that, given the existing cost of acquiring a car, the mobility allowance alone, even assuming possible increases in its rate, was not, and would not be, sufficient to enable disabled people without other resources to obtain one. This would be a particularly acute problem for newly-disabled people who had just begun to receive the allowance.

In the case of disabled people who could drive, the trike and the assistance which went with it represented a good deal more than the provision for mobility which the allowance on its own could offer. This led to public anxiety about those who might have had a trike if the vehicle scheme had continued, but, in spite of having the mobility allowance and needing a car, could not afford to obtain one. The same anxiety extended to the newly admitted non-drivers, who expected that the allowance would enable them to obtain a car in which they could be driven by friends or relatives.

Thus, although in general disabled people's organisations welcomed the mobility allowance, there was serious concern because it was not sufficient to provide a car on the road, free of charge, as the vehicle scheme had, at any rate for drivers. This was against the background of pressure on the Government for some years after the introduction of the mobility allowance, to bring back the trike and/or to provide a replacement vehicle for it as an optional alternative to the allowance. In the light of the developments described below, this has now subsided.

The RADAR initiative

These concerns led to an initiative by the Royal Association for Disability and Rehabilitation (RADAR). The Government had asked the Central Council for the Disabled, RADAR's predecessor, to set up a working party to look into the mobility allowance and how it could best be used. The working party made a number of recommendations to improve the allowance, many of which have now been implemented. In particular, because of the concerns about its limited purchasing power, they proposed a scheme whereby the allowance could be used to lease a new car, analogous to fleet hire in the commercial sphere. To enable this proposal to be developed, the Government made a grant to RADAR to pay for the preparation of such a scheme.

The Scheme developed in collaboration with Leyland Cars and the United Dominions Trust (UDT), in which George

Wilson (RADAR's Director) played a leading part, called for a leasing payment by the disabled person for four years, equal to the full amount of the mobility allowance, paid direct to UDT. However, it also required a payment from the Department to UDT, possibly rising to £5,000,000 a year, to bridge the gap between the income from the mobility allowance and the full cost of the leases.

Additional lump sum payments (rising to about £1,000,000 a year) were required from the Department to meet the capital cost of automatic transmission and/or conversion to hand controls, where these were needed. The only car to be provided was an 850cc Mini. There was to be a free recovery service and free provision of a hired car if the leased car was off the road for repair after a breakdown. RADAR also proposed a secondary scheme of assistance with purchase or hire purchase.

The Government, although grateful to RADAR for their pioneer work in developing the concept of leasing in return for the mobility allowance, came to the conclusion that a scheme involving commercial arrangements for the acquisition of cars, but with direct subsidies from public funds, was in principle undesirable, and in any case did not go far enough, since it did not allow a choice of car.

THE APPROACH TO LORD GOODMAN

The Government remained determined to find a solution to the problem, and concluded that, in principle, an effective and acceptable solution was more likely to be found through an arrangement outside Government than through introducing a new and direct State scheme – even though it was now apparent that any viable scheme could not be entirely commercial.

As a first step, Lord Ennals decided to invite the help of Lord Goodman, who had recently assisted the Department in negotiations with the medical profession. In discussion with him there emerged the possibility of setting up a leasing scheme on preferential terms which would bring the acquisition of a car within the reach of most people with the mobility allowance, but which would be backed up by charitable help for those for whom the allowance and their other resources were insufficient for the particular car they needed.

Lord Goodman agreed to explore a scheme on these lines, and he immediately enlisted the financial and fundraising skills of Mr Jeffrey (now Lord) Sterling. Together they devised the charity which was to become known as Motability, and a leasing scheme to be operated by a special company, Motability Finance Limited (MFL), working exclusively for Motability. MFL was set up by a consortium of the clearing banks, and we owe the successful launching of this innovative venture very largely to Lord Sterling and Mr (now Sir John) Quinton of Barclays Bank. Their part in the setting up of MFL and its later development are described in Chapter 4.

There were many others who contributed to the successful development of Motability by becoming members of the charity at a large meeting convened by a telegram from Lord Goodman. Those present included Lord Drogheda and Sir Douglas Bader.

The formation of Motability* was announced to the House of Commons on 6 December 1977 by Lord Ennals, and was welcomed by Mr Patrick (now Lord) Jenkin on behalf of the Opposition. The all-party support then expressed has continued throughout Motability's existence, and has been a source of great encouragement to the charity. The constitution of the charity and its governors are explained in Chapter 12.

The press notice issued on the same day by the Department of Health and Social Security explained that Motability would supplement, and not duplicate, State provisions, and would in no way impinge on the independence of those who were helped. It also made it clear that it would be entirely for disabled people themselves to decide whether they wanted to

---

*Commenting on the announcement, the *Guardian* newspaper said in a leading article: 'Motability – surely a name which could only have been invented by a political adviser!' The name was in fact devised by a civil servant.

use Motability's facilities or to use their mobility allowance in some other way. These statements expressed, and still express, essential elements in Motability's policy.

LORD GOODMAN CH

Motability learned with great regret of the death of Lord Goodman, its Life President, in May 1995 at the age of 81. It is sad that he was unable to take part in the celebration of the delivery of Motability's 500,000th car in July 1995, marking a most important milestone in the development of the charity.

Motability benefited greatly from Lord Goodman's inspiring leadership during the 18 years from its formation to the time of his death. In particular, it recalls with gratitude his immediate response in 1977, as described above, and with the support of Lord Sterling, to the request of the Government to set up a scheme which would make it possible for disabled people to use their mobility allowance to obtain a car. The very large number of people who have since taken the road to freedom of mobility through Motability have reason to be grateful for that response.

It is pleasing to know that among his many achievements in a long and distinguished career, Lord Goodman singled out the establishment of Motability as having given him the greatest satisfaction.

2

SETTING UP MOTABILITY

The Motability Scheme, which has been described by Lord Goodman as a splendid example of a mixed economy, has no parallel in any country in the world. It is a joint enterprise of the Department of Social Security, voluntary effort represented by Motability, the clearing banks, motor manufacturers and dealers, insurance companies and the motoring associations. Other contributors are the mobility centres which advise on the needs of disabled drivers and passengers, and the specialists who provide the adaptations to standard vehicles and the special vehicles needed by many of Motability's customers.

The negotiations which led up to the formation of Motability were principally conducted by Lord Sterling, always with the advice and support of Lord Goodman; from the Department, Sir Patrick Nairne (Permanent Secretary) and Allan Beard (the Under-Secretary responsible for trikes); and Sir John Quinton on behalf of the banks. The negotiations were carried out with the full backing of the Secretary of State, Lord Ennals, and the Minister for the Disabled, Lord Morris. The division of responsibilities which was then agreed between the parties concerned, and has remained unchanged, is described below.

Motability

Motability would establish an office which would be responsible for making the leasing scheme known to all mobility allowance recipients (the issue of the information being undertaken by the Department) and for the handling of applications

12

and renewal applications for cars, up to and including the contract with the dealer. This would include advice, where necessary, on the choice of the car, and any adaptations needed.

Motability would raise funds for the assistance of people whose mobility allowance alone was insufficient to obtain the car they needed under the leasing scheme, and would investigate and determine applications for grants from these funds. (There has been some confusion between the funds and the administration grant from the Department. Some people have wrongly assumed that this grant is available to assist disabled people directly, whereas it can only be used to meet the costs of Motability. The Department has made very substantial contributions separately to Motability's own funds – see below.)

Motability would deal with all initial enquiries by telephone or letter about the Scheme and the issue of detailed information about it.

The banks

The clearing banks would establish a company, Motability Finance Limited (MFL), working solely for Motability, and would provide it with funds, on agreed terms, for the purchase of cars to be leased under the Motability Scheme. These arrangements were later extended to hire purchase. Jointly with Motability, MFL would negotiate terms with motor manufacturers and dealers for the supply of cars, and with an insurance company for the insurance of the leased cars.

MFL would be responsible for operating the leasing arrangements in each case after the settlement of the contract with the dealer, including payments for maintenance, early termination of leases, etc.

The Department

The Department would pay a grant for the administrative expenses of the Motability office (including the cost of

13

operating a scheme of charitable grants), such that the charitable funds raised by Motability could be devoted entirely to assisting disabled people with their mobility. (For the first year the grant also covered the expenses of fundraising.) This undertaking was honoured in full by successive Governments from 1977 until 1995 (see Chapter 15 for subsequent developments). The grant rose from £204,633 in 1978–79, the first full year, to £4,646,000 in 1996–97, matching the remarkable growth in Motability's work.

With the customer's agreement, the Department would pay over direct to MFL the mobility allowance of each disabled person participating in the leasing scheme. The assurance of these payments would overcome the problem that most recipients of the mobility allowance would otherwise present an unacceptable credit risk.

CONCESSIONS BY THE GOVERNMENT

The participation of the Department in these arrangements called for a number of concessions which involved a good deal of negotiation, both internally and with the Treasury. The first was the agreement to pay over the mobility allowance of a disabled person participating in the leasing scheme direct to MFL. This had of course the great advantage of guaranteeing the payments to MFL without any question of credit ratings and cutting out all collecting costs, so substantially improving the terms which MFL could offer. But it ran contrary to the general principle of the inalienability of Social Security benefits, and so was a considerable concession.

Secondly, it is a general principle regulating Government assistance to voluntary organisations that the grant-in-aid of their administration is not 100 per cent, thus giving them an incentive to efficiency and to raising part of the cost themselves. The Department recognised, however, that it was in the interests of the Government to allow Motability to devote the whole of its own income to assisting disabled people with grants – the more successful it was in this aim,

14

the greater would be the success of the mobility allowance scheme. As a result, until 1995 the administration grant covered Motability's approved expenses in full, excluding the cost of fundraising.

Finally, there was the question of the rate of mobility allowance. The Treasury were initially concerned that the allowance, only a minority of whose recipients were expected to use Motability's services, would be automatically linked to the cost of motoring, which might well rise by a greater amount than the Retail Prices Index (RPI), the general criterion for increases in Social Security benefits. (The mobility allowance was not, however, statutorily linked with the Index.) They were reassured on this point, but the Government nevertheless increased the allowance from its original level of £4 to £5 in November 1976, and to £7 in November 1977. It then took the bold step, announced by Lord Ennals when he informed Parliament of the setting up of Motability, of raising the rate to £10 in July 1978, thus doubling it within a year. (This large increase was undoubtedly given to make it possible to develop a viable leasing scheme. Since that date annual upratings have brought the level of the allowance to £34.60 in April 1997.

In announcing the increase to be made in the allowance from July 1978, Lord Ennals said that in future there would be annual upratings, beginning in November 1979, and that the allowance would be protected against inflation. This was not a statutory provision, but the new disability living allowance, which incorporates the mobility allowance, is however linked by statute with the RPI. Upratings now take place in April.

Before agreeing to participate, the clearing banks had to obtain the approval of the financial authorities, because of the 'corset' then operating, to the provision of up to £100,000,000 for MFL. The negotiations with the banks are described more fully in Chapter 4.

All these concessions, coupled with the advantageous terms provided by MFL, have made it possible for Motability to offer cars more cheaply than disabled people can normally obtain elsewhere.

15

SETTING UP THE MOTABILITY OFFICE

In order to fulfil its part in the agreed responsibilities, Motability needed to establish a staff and an office. Lord Goodman asked the Department to provide a civil servant to undertake this work, and in 1977 Barry James, a Principal in the Department, accepted an invitation to be seconded in order to set up the charity. He arranged for premises to be provided in a Departmental building in London, State House in High Holborn, and set about creating an entirely new organisation, completing the recruitment of staff by June 1978. The pay and conditions of service of the staff (who were not civil servants) were modelled on those of local authority staff.

Barry was ideally suited to his new task, having played a leading part in setting up and operating another Government benefit for disabled people, the attendance allowance. Motability owes a great debt of gratitude to him for the enthusiastic and efficient way in which he responded to the challenge of his new and unique task. In particular, he established the close working relationships with the Department which were essential for the success of the Scheme, including arrangements for the payment of mobility allowances to MFL. His collaboration with Harry Hall of MFL, who also made a most valuable contribution to the creation of the leasing scheme, was especially successful.

ESTABLISHING THE LEASING SCHEME

The leasing scheme was launched on 15 June 1978 at a press conference at the House of Commons, attended by Ministers. The first applications for cars were received in June 1978, and the first cars were put on the road on 25 July 1978, the participating manufacturers being British Leyland (now Rover), Chrysler (now Peugeot), Ford and Vauxhall.

One of the essential factors in the establishment of the Scheme was the willingness of these manufacturers to take the risk of entering what was at the time an untried scheme. They

16

would have been unlikely to have done so if there had not been the financial commitment of the banks and the personal authority of Lord Goodman and Lord Sterling – and if the Government had not decided to combine its financial backing through the mobility allowance with freedom for the Scheme from the constraints of direct Government involvement.

The Zurich Insurance Company was appointed as insurer of the fleet of leased cars, and for many years provided a valuable service. Motability is grateful to this company for undertaking the insurance – it was the only company approached by the brokers which was prepared to enter a field with considerable risk on acceptable terms.

Because of the work involved, invitations to allowance recipients to apply for Motability Scheme cars could not be issued all at once, and it was decided to phase them in by age group, giving priority to 16-year-olds and moving upwards in age bands. The issue of invitations was completed by September 1979. In July 1979 invitations to apply for cars on hire purchase by age group began to be issued, phased in with the current age group for leasing invitations.

In January 1981 hire purchase of powered wheelchairs over a two-year term was offered, and in October 1981 hire purchase of used cars over a two- or three-year term.

THE CONCERNS OF DISABLED PEOPLE

As mentioned in Chapter 1, although disabled people generally welcomed the Motability Scheme, there was some misgiving as to whether it would manage to provide mobility on the road, virtually free of charge, as the trike scheme had. There was in particular opposition in some quarters to any reliance on charitable funds, instead of direct help from the Government, to top up the mobility allowance when it was insufficient to meet all the costs of obtaining and running a car. This concern was to be largely removed in later years by the Government's decision to contribute to the Tenth Anniversary Trust Fund and to make further grants for

17

special cases in the form of the Mobility Equipment and Drivers Funds (see Chapter 8).

TEMPORARY SUSPENSIONS

In 1979 it was necessary to suspend the operation of the leasing scheme because of uncertainty about the amount of the next uprating of mobility allowance. This was only a brief interruption, however, and resumption was made possible by the remission of VAT on the purchase price of cars referred to above. A similar situation occurred in 1984 following the reduction of relief on first-year tax allowances, but trading was quickly renewed in the same year with the removal of VAT on leasing payments in new cases.

BENEFICIAL CHANGES MADE BY GOVERNMENT

In the early years of the charity, the Government made a number of valuable changes for the benefit of disabled people which enabled Motability to improve the terms it could offer to its customers. The impressive list of these changes, and of those made by successive Governments in later years, many of them in response to representations from Motability, is set out below.

1978   People with mobility allowance exempted from Vehicle Excise Duty – i.e. they no longer required a tax disc

1979   Remission of VAT on the purchase price of cars leased to disabled people

Upper age limit for the first award of mobility allowance raised to 65 for women (previously it was their pensionable age of 60)

Mobility allowance to continue for ten years after age 65 if awarded before that age

1980   Motability Schemes protected from the reduction in capital allowance on leased cars

1981   VAT removed from car adaptations and electric wheelchairs
        Reduction to 16 in the age limit for disabled drivers
1982   Mobility allowance exempted from Income Tax
1984   VAT removed from leasing payments for Motability cars
1988   £5,000,000 provided by the Government for the Tenth Anniversary Trust Fund (see Chapter 8)
1989   Car tax removed from Motability cars bought for contract hire (leasing). The resulting reduction in leasing costs brought about a 50 per cent increase in the number of cars supplied.
        Mobility allowance to continue to age 80 if awarded before age 65
1990   Certain deaf/blind people made eligible for mobility allowance
1991   Car tax no longer repayable on early termination of Motability contract hire agreements (previously, exemption from this tax was removed retrospectively in these circumstances)
        £3,000,000 over three years donated by the Government for the Mobility Equipment Fund
        People without both legs automatically entitled to mobility allowance
1992   Mobility component of disability living allowance (DLA)* to continue to be paid indefinitely if awarded before age 65
        A further £6,000,000 over three years (1993–1995) provided by the Government for the Mobility Equipment Fund
1993   A further £1,000,000 a year for three years, beginning in April 1994, provided by the Government, to be

* The new DLA, introduced in 1992, included the equivalent of the previously separate mobility allowance.

	used for wheelchair drivers needing especially expensive equipment (the Drivers Fund)
1994	The Department agreed to an increase in Motability's administration grant to enable the charity to enlarge its organisation to keep pace with the growth in its work and to introduce more professional standards
	Motability contract hire vehicles exempted from the new insurance premium tax
1995	Existing Motability Scheme users exempted from restrictions on the continuation of the DLA affecting hospital in-patients
1998	Disabled drivers, or appointed nominees, with exemption from vehicle excise duty exempted from the new £25 first registration fee.

Some of these changes have benefited mobility allowance recipients in general, but the removal of car tax on leased cars in 1989 was of especial benefit to those using Motability's schemes. As mentioned above, the resulting reduction in lease charges produced a large rise in the number of applications and of cars supplied by Motability.

The changes reflect the support and encouragement which Motability has received from Social Security Ministers, especially those already referred to, but particular mention should be made of the great help received in recent years from The Rt Hon Sir Nicholas Scott KBE JP the former Minister for Social Security and Disabled People.

THE GROWTH IN THE SUPPLY OF VEHICLES

After an initial period of uncertainty while the Schemes were becoming known, there has been a rapidly increasing growth in the number of vehicles supplied each year by Motability. This is illustrated by the year by year figures in Appendix 1.

Over the period from July 1978 to the end of December 1997, Motability supplied the following numbers of vehicles:

Cars on hire	752,517
New cars on HP	73,138
Used cars on HP	24,783
Wheelchairs	20,262
Total	870,700

Many of the cars on hire were supplied to people taking out a second or subsequent agreement, so that the figure of cars on hire does not represent the number of *individuals* who have hired a car since 1978. However, on a conservative estimate the number of individual people who have acquired a car through one or other of Motability's schemes is now probably over 500,000.

The growth in the number of people receiving the allowance is shown in Appendix 2. It was undoubtedly affected by the assimilation of the mobility allowance into the DLA in April 1992.

The DLA has two components – a care component, and a mobility component which superseded the mobility allowance. The mobility component is payable at one of two rates – a lower rate or a higher rate (currently £13.15 and £34.60 respectively). The higher rate continued at the same level as the mobility allowance, and is awarded on the same criteria. The rate of the DLA, unlike that of the mobility allowance, is linked statutorily to the Retail Prices Index.

The lower rate of the mobility component is insufficient to enable the recipient to participate in the Motability Schemes, so the introduction of the extended benefit did not in itself affect the number of people applying to Motability. The extensive publicity given to the DLA, however, led to increased applications for the benefit, and so to more applications for cars. The growth in the number of DLA recipients is expected to continue, even if not at the hitherto remarkable rate.

3

THE DEVELOPMENT OF THE
MOTABILITY SCHEMES

Since 1977 Motability has developed four schemes for disabled people receiving the higher rate mobility component of the disability living allowance.* (In general, what is said here about this component applies also to the war pensioners' mobility supplement – see Chapter 6.) These schemes provide:

New cars on contract hire
New cars on hire purchase
Used cars on hire purchase
Powered wheelchairs and scooters on hire purchase

In the case of cars, it has always been for a disabled person wishing to apply to the Motability Scheme to choose which of the three schemes to use, although in certain circumstances where a grant is applied for, the award of the grant may be made conditional upon using a particular method. The development of the four schemes is described overleaf.

* The mobility component of the disability living allowance has replaced the mobility allowance referred to in earlier chapters. This component may be at one of two rates. Only people with the higher rate may participate in Motability's schemes. For simplicity, 'allowance' is used hereafter to mean a disability living allowance which includes a mobility component at the higher rate.

NEW CARS ON CONTRACT HIRE

This was the original Motability Scheme, starting in 1978. It was at first referred to as leasing, leases being for four years. This period was soon changed to three years. The Scheme provides a new car, serviced, repaired, comprehensively insured and with roadside assistance. It is used by some 90 per cent of the people who obtain vehicles through the Motability Scheme.

The disabled person does not have to be a driver to enter the Scheme. He or she can hire a car as a passenger and nominate up to two assistants or family members as the drivers. Children from five years old can qualify for a car as passengers, provided that they are in receipt of the allowance.

Anyone who has an allowance with more than three years to run at the time of signing can enter into a hire agreement. In certain circumstances, allowance recipients can enter into a joint agreement for one car.

Cars can be supplied only by a dealer who has been appointed by the car manufacturer and MFL to deal with Motability. In December 1997, 21 manufacturers were participating, each offering up to 20 models: Citroën, Daewoo, Daihatsu, Fiat, Ford, Hyundai, Kia, Mazda, Nissan, Peugeot, Renault, Rover, Saab, Seat, Skoda, Subaru, Suzuki, Toyota, Vauxhall, Volkswagen and Volvo.

Vehicles converted to allow passengers to travel in their wheelchairs are also available through Brotherwood, Gowrings Mobility, Lewis Reed, Universal Mobility, and Widnes Car Centre.

Unfortunately, car prices are generally subject to increases every few months. During the interval between the date of the agreement and the delivery of the car, the customer is protected against any such increases by the holding of the advance payment and weekly rental for three months. Conversely, if the price is reduced customers can benefit from the lower price.

Cars used exclusively by or for the purposes of a disabled person in receipt of an allowance have been exempt from vehicle excise duty – the road fund licence – since 1978. (This applies also to cars obtained under the hire purchase schemes described below.)

Rental charges

Once a customer has signed an agreement the rental remains fixed and cannot be increased during its term, no matter what happens to prevailing financial conditions. This provides security to disabled people, particularly against inflation or increases in tax or interest rates.

Where the regular payments of the allowance to MFL are insufficient to cover the full cost of the lease, an advance payment is required. However, in December 1997, 99 models of car were available without such a payment, including 13 with automatic transmission.

In most cases the whole of the allowance, £34.60 a week as at January 1998, including uprating increases, is paid over to MFL by the Benefits Agency. By December 1997, however, improvements in the terms of the leasing scheme, particularly insurance costs, had made it possible for Motability's price list to show 19 manufacturers offering a total of 45 models in return for a constant rental throughout the agreement, in most cases somewhat less than the full amount of the allowance.

At the end of 1997 some 24 per cent of leases were at constant rentals, and 31 with no advance payment. Where the rental is less than the allowance, the balance, including uprating increases, is paid regularly to the customer by the Benefits Agency.

At the end of the hire period another new car may be hired. Customers coming to the end of an agreement are told six months in advance that if they wish to renew they will need to apply in good time, so that arrangements can be made to ensure that there is no interruption of their mobility. The great majority of customers do obtain another vehicle in this way.

Alternatively, the customer may be able to come to an arrangement with the dealer to buy the previously hired car, although this forms no part of the hire agreement and neither Motability nor MFL takes part in the sale. The transaction can, however, be financed through the Motability used car hire purchase scheme, subject to the conditions on page 29.

Adaptations

If necessary, the car can be adapted to suit the particular needs of the disabled person, provided that the adaptations are easily removable at the end of the agreement. There are now several firms which specialise in the production and fitting of adaptations. The most common are hand-controlled brakes and accelerators, steering-wheel knobs, pedal guards, extended switches, raised or rotating seats, car top hoists for drivers or passengers, and seat harnesses. The cost of adaptations has to be added to the advance hire payment, if any, and the adaptations must be removed at the user's expense at the end of the hire period before the car is returned to the dealer. For this reason, if major adaptations are needed, hire purchase may be a better option, or in a limited number of cases, five-year hire agreements.

Automatic transmission and/or power-assisted steering are normally factory fitted and included in the cost of the car. If the disabled person has exceptionally restricted power in his or her arms, the power steering may have to be specially lightened.

Assistance with costs

If the customer cannot afford the advance payment and/or the cost of adaptations, help may be given from Motability's charitable fund or the Mobility Equipment or Drivers Funds (see Chapter 9) for the least expensive suitable vehicle. Where appropriate, grants are made for five-year leases. Assistance can also be given with the cost of driving lessons.

Insurance

Insurance of leased cars has always been on fleet basis – i.e. with a uniform premium (subject to what is said on page 26) without a no-claim bonus. The premiums are the same for every customer, irrespective of age, sex, financial status, location or disability – insurance on an individual basis would require a prohibitively expensive premium for new and younger drivers and for those living in high-risk areas. Drivers with consistently bad driving and claims records may be excluded from the Scheme.

The policy includes loss-of-use cover if the car is unusable for more than one week because of mechanical breakdown or accidental damage. It provides a weekly payment, after the first seven days, and for up to six weeks, equivalent to the weekly allowance, provided that a courtesy vehicle has not been provided.

A steep rise in insurance premiums in October 1991 made it necessary to introduce ways of reducing costs for the generality of customers. It was decided that from May 1992 there should be a compulsory £75 excess for accidental damage, plus an additional excess of £25 for all drivers under 25 and/or with less than one year's driving experience, and an additional £50 for drivers under 21. A total of two people, one of whom may be the disabled person, may now be listed as drivers at no additional cost, but a charge of £150 is made for a third driver, unless there are exceptional circumstances requiring additional drivers – e.g. where there are a number of carers looking after a disabled passenger. Measures were also agreed to increase inspections of vehicles incurring damage claims, and to review the claims records of drivers before allowing another vehicle on contract hire.

In 1994 the Government agreed to exempt Motability contract hire vehicles from the newly introduced insurance premium tax.

Until 1990, part of the insurance premium was collected by means of a separate payment, but after that date MFL were able to provide an agreement whereby the whole of the premium was covered by the payment of the customer's mobility allowance. As a result, customers were saved the necessity of budgeting for insurance costs each year.

As mentioned above, lower lease rentals were made possible

in 1995 by reductions in insurance costs. These applied to agreements entered into after 30 September 1995. In addition, customers who hired a car between 1 October 1993 and that date were eligible for a cash rebate on the insurance element of the lease rental. MFL was made responsible for the administration of the rental rebates to customers.

Emergency assistance

The Motability Scheme provides full membership of the RAC, giving roadside assistance, Homestart, Relay and Relay Plus. The RAC took over the contract for this service from the AA for new agreements from 1 October 1997.

Mileage charges and tyres

Charges are made if the average annual mileage exceeds 12,000. (Originally this limit was 10,000 and it was applied to each year without averaging.) The average mileage of Motability users during the contract hire period is 24,000. For all cars, the first four tyres are replaced free of charge.

Wear and tear on contract hire vehicles

A guide has been issued to contract hire customers, clarifying what constitutes fair wear and tear as opposed to abuse or neglect of the vehicle. This is important, because a re-purchase agent may decline to take back a vehicle if it is damaged beyond fair wear and tear and the cost of repair is not covered by insurance. In such circumstances, the customer may be called upon to pay for the repair.

Customers' handbook

A handbook is issued to participating customers, explaining their rights and obligations under the contract hire scheme.

NEW CARS ON HIRE PURCHASE

This scheme began in 1979, a little later than contract hire, as part of Motability's policy of giving the customer the maximum possible choice of ways of obtaining a car.

Anyone who has an allowance with more than four years to run, whether passenger or driver, can enter into a hire purchase agreement with MFL over four or five years.

The agreement can cover virtually any model of new car from the manufacturers participating in the contract hire scheme, and from 10 other suppliers of new cars in the UK. Special rear-access vehicles for passengers, and adaptations if necessary, can be included. Motability and MFL have negotiated substantial discounts with the manufacturers.

All or part of the allowance will be paid over to MFL to meet the cost of the monies borrowed, which will depend on the cost of the car after the payment of an initial deposit, which is always required. If only part of the allowance is needed for the hire purchase instalments, the balance is paid direct to the disabled person, as are the annual increases in the rate of the allowance during the period of the agreement. Fully comprehensive insurance, maintenance and repairs, any necessary adaptations and membership of motoring organisations are the responsibility of the customer. Motability is able to suggest the names of brokers specialising in insurance for disabled people. One of the benefits of hire purchase is that there is no mileage limit.

Motability, MFL and Royal & Sun Alliance are at present examining the possibility of a voluntary scheme for the insurance on favourable terms of cars being bought on hire purchase.

Some of the adaptations which may be required have been described above in the section on contract hire, but the more extensive adaptations, such as joystick steering and specially converted vehicles, can only be provided for in a hire purchase agreement.

Help may be given from Motability's charitable fund or the Mobility Equipment or Drivers Funds with the initial deposit and cost of adaptations for the least expensive suitable car, where hire purchase is considered to be preferable to contract hire. Provided that the customer can afford to pay for insurance and maintenance, this may sometimes be the best option for both Motability and the customer – otherwise an application for a further grant would be needed at the end of a contract hire period. Grants may also be made for driving lessons.

USED CARS ON HIRE PURCHASE

This scheme began in 1982 as a further increase in the choices offered to disabled people. There was considerable and understandable reluctance by the banks and MFL to being involved in dealing in used cars, and it is to their credit that they finally approved the Scheme.

The Scheme is open to passengers as well as drivers. The customer is able to shop around for the most suitable car and price, and then, subject to the dealer being on MFL's approved list, to apply to Motability to buy it. The hire purchase agreement with MFL is for two or three years, and the customer must have an allowance award for at least the duration of the agreement. In most cases the used car, adapted if necessary, must be under five years old, have done less than 60,000 miles, and pass an inspection under special arrangements made with the AA. The fee for the inspection is included in the cost of the HP agreement – the customer does not have to find the cost in advance. If the inspection reveals that serious repairs are required i.e. those of a safety or security nature the dealer is expected to pay the re-inspection fee. Major improvements in the Scheme were made in 1996, including a wider choice of cars, revised warranty cover, and more comprehensive inspection of cars, including a valuation service.

As with the hire purchase of new cars, any part of the allowance not required for the hire purchase instalments is paid direct by the Benefits Agency to the customer, together with the annual increases in the allowance. Insurance, maintenance and repairs are the responsibility of the customer, but AA Mechanical Breakdown Insurance is provided from the date that the customer takes delivery of the car. RAC membership and attendant benefits are also covered by the agreement.

THE SCHEMES COMPARED

The main differences between the three car schemes can be summarised as follows:

Contract hire

- The car is never owned by the customer. When the agreement period ends, it is returned to the dealer or maintenance agent.
- In most cases, the whole of the customer's allowance, including any subsequent uprating increases, is paid to MFL by the Benefits Agency for the term of the agreement. (In some cases, as explained above, the payment is fixed throughout the term, and it may be less than the full amount of the allowance.) In addition, an advance payment by the customer may be required.
- The cost of servicing and repairs is included.
- Comprehensive insurance cover for two nominated drivers is included, regardless of the area in which the customer lives. It is subject to an excess, depending on the person's age and driving experience.
- Mileage above an average of 12,000 a year will incur an excess mileage charge.
- Adaptations to the car are restricted to those that can be removed, at reasonable cost, at the end of the hire period.

Hire purchase of new cars

- The customer will own the car, but not until the end of the hire purchase period.
- Depending on the car chosen, a deposit will be required, and in addition a fixed part of the allowance is paid to MFL by the Benefits Agency for the term of the agreement.

The balance, including increases at upratings, is paid to the customer by the Agency.

- The customer must pay separately for fully comprehensive insurance. No other insurance is provided, and no roadside assistance.
- The customer pays for maintenance and repairs.
- There are no mileage restrictions.
- There are no restrictions on the adaptations to be fitted.

Hire purchase of used cars

- There must be a satisfactory inspection of the car before the application.
- The customer will own the car, but not until the end of the hire purchase period.
- Depending on the car chosen, a fixed part of the allowance is paid to MFL by the Benefits Agency for the term of the agreement. The balance, including any uprating increases, is paid to the customer by the Benefits Agency.
- The customer must pay for fully comprehensive insurance.
- The customer pays for maintenance and repairs, but AA Mechanical Breakdown Insurance, covering the cost of repairing some car components, is included.
- RAC membership and attendant benefits are included.
- There are no mileage charges.
- There are no restrictions on the adaptations to be fitted.
- A deposit must be paid to the dealer.

POWERED WHEELCHAIRS ON HIRE PURCHASE

Only very limited categories of people can be supplied with powered wheelchairs under the National Health Service, although the Department has recently announced changes, which include a voucher scheme, which may make more people eligible. For people with an allowance who are not so entitled, Motability has offered a hire purchase scheme since 1981 for powered wheelchairs and scooters. A discount of five per cent

31

off retail prices has been negotiated with seven manufacturers. The hire purchase term is for two or three years, and the customer must have an allowance award for at least the term of the agreement. There is at present a minimum deposit of £200. Any difference between the instalment payable and the current rate of the allowance (including uprating increases) is paid direct to the customer by the Benefits Agency.

Discussions are at present taking place with manufacturers with a view to improving the terms on which wheelchairs are supplied. The First Class Suppliers Charter (see Chapter 15), which sets minimum operating standards for dealers, was extended to wheelchair suppliers in July 1997. It has already been agreed that there will be buy-back arrangements if an agreement is ended through death.

EARLY TERMINATION OF AGREEMENTS

As explained below (see Chapter 4), the Motability Scheme bears the loss on the premature termination of contract hire or hire purchase agreements i.e. where there is a loss on the resale of the car if there are bona fide reasons for the termination, such as the death or increased disability of the customer, or where a driver is no longer available to assist a disabled passenger. In such cases, payment of the allowance to the customer is resumed by the Benefits Agency, unless another agreement is entered into. In other cases, any loss on the car has to be borne by the customer.

RETENTION OF THE ALLOWANCE

There are powers in Regulations made by the Secretary of State for Social Services*, enabling the Benefits Agency to continue paying the allowance to MFL in certain circum-

---

* SI (1987), No. 1986

stances where there are outstanding debts e.g. if the car is not returned at the due time, or if the car is unreasonably returned before the end of the agreement. In practice, these powers are rarely used.

SHORT ALLOWANCE AWARDS

As explained above, an agreement cannot be entered into with MFL unless the period of award of the allowance extends beyond the end of the prospective agreement i.e. it is for more than three to five years, depending on its type. In cases where a notice of award is not produced, it is therefore necessary for Motability to ask the Benefits Agency about the period of award. Special arrangements have been set up to clear these enquiries as quickly as possible.

If the award is of insufficient length i.e. it will not be effective for at least the term of the prospective agreement plus eight weeks, an agreement cannot normally be entered into, and the customer will be asked to make a 'shortfall' payment to Motability. This will be the weekly payment for the vehicle multiplied by the number of weeks for which the award is short of the contractual term, plus eight weeks. The eight week period allows for the administration of the contract, insurance cover and vehicle ordering and preparation.

If the 'shortfall' period is for more than six months or less than two weeks, the customer is advised instead to consider an appeal to the Department for an award extension, bearing in mind the risk that such an appeal could possibly lead to the loss of the allowance. If this situation occurs where a grant has been asked for to obtain a car, it may be possible to provide the required contribution as part of the grant.

PERIODS IN HOSPITAL

Under changes made from 31 July 1996, payment of the allowance is suspended after 28 days of free hospital in-patient treatment (84 days for children). However, by a special dispensation people with existing Motability agreements will continue to receive sufficient benefit to meet the terms of their agreement for its full term. Unfortunately, in spite of representations by Motability and other organisations, this does not apply to those wishing to enter into an agreement (except for a wheel-chair) who have not done so before entering hospital. Recipients of the war pensioners' mobility supplement are not affected by these regulations.

INFORMATION FOR PROSPECTIVE CUSTOMERS

A short introductory leaflet about the Motability Schemes is issued by the Benefits Agency to every allowance recipient on first award of the allowance and on each renewal of the order book. This invites the recipient to ask for more information about Motability's schemes by filling in the reply coupon. If this is returned Motability despatches a comprehensive application booklet, explaining all the Schemes.

In 1991 and 1992 a 24-page illustrated guide was issued to all allowance recipients, giving much fuller information than in previous publicity material about Motability's schemes, and including advice on the choice of a car and adaptations. The cost of the guide was met by paid advertisements by car manufacturers, and it was sent by the Benefits Agency to all recipients of the allowance, except those who had asked not to receive it. As a result, there was a large increase in applications for cars and in enquiries to manufacturers and dealers.

VEHICLES SUPPLIED

The Schemes are demand-led, and because of the attractiveness of the contract hire scheme it has experienced very high growth, averaging around 20 per cent per annum in the last five years. In less than five years it has doubled in size. The proportion of allowance recipients over the year who have chosen to participate in one of the Motability Schemes is shown in Appendix 2 – at the end of 1997 it was 22.4 per cent.

By the end of 1997 over 870,000 cars had been supplied through MFL, and the fleet of cars i.e. those covered by current contract hire and HP agreements, was over 340,000. Detailed figures of the cars and wheelchairs supplied year by year from 1978 onwards are given in Appendix 1.

4

THE DEVELOPING ROLE OF
MOTABILITY FINANCE LIMITED

THE APPROACH TO THE CLEARING BANKS

In 1977, following the Government's request to Lord
Goodman to develop a scheme to enable disabled people to
acquire personal transport, Lord Goodman and Mr Jeffrey
(now Lord) Sterling consulted Mr (now Sir John) Quinton,
subsequently Chairman of Barclays Bank, about the possibility
of help from the clearing banks in financing the purchase of
cars for leasing to disabled people in return for their mobility
allowance.

At the time Sir John was a recently appointed General
Manager of Barclays Bank, and also Deputy Chairman of
Mercantile Credit. It was highly relevant that Mercantile
Credit had introduced leasing into the UK in the 1960s and
were still regarded as leading the UK leasing market.

It was explained that the mobility allowance would be at the
rate of no more than £10 a week initially, and that the average
purchase price of a new car would be about £1,850. The aim
was to obtain finance for the Scheme at rates significantly
cheaper than those obtainable on the open market. The
proposal was that the banks should set up a company, which
they would own and operate, dedicated to the provision of
Motability Scheme cars.

At this time Sir Anthony Tuke, Chairman of Barclays, was

the Chairman of the Committee of London and Scottish Clearing Banks. After consulting him, and with his approval, Sir John Quinton began discussions with the banks. Lord Goodman's suggestion that they might need to lend a total of £100,000,000 – a very large sum at the time – was not greeted initially with much enthusiasm. Moreover, to provide this capital at something under cost, as was at first suggested by Lord Goodman, would mean lending at less than the rates charged by the banks even to their best customers, when for leasing transactions a margin well above that figure would be expected. The banks were therefore being asked to forgo several million pounds of profit – a contribution to a single charity far greater than they gave to any other individual cause. The banks have long given substantial sums and practical assistance to many charities – for example, over £10,000,000 in the year in which they were asked to help Motability – but this is spread between hundreds of different causes.

The banks made two important prior stipulations. The first was that any scheme would have the support of all political parties i.e. that there would be no risk of substantial change on a change of Government, and this assurance was readily given after consultation with those concerned. The second was that the Department should agree to clear-cut arrangements for the assignment of participating disabled people's mobility allowances to the new company i.e. that there should be no question of the company having to investigate credit ratings or apply pressure for payment of the leasing charges. As explained in Chapter 2, arrangements on these lines were agreed by the Department.

Eventually the banks decided that a scheme was feasible, and a formula was agreed with Lord Goodman whereby funds of up to £100,000,000 would be provided to enable the charity to provide cars for disabled people. It was also agreed that the banks would forgo some profit, to ensure that in practice disabled people would receive a distinctly more favourable leasing deal than would otherwise be available. However, it was never intended that the banks should forgo all profit. As already explained, they could not countenance so large an amount going in this way to one charity – donations which did not simply come out of their shareholders' profits, but derived in the ultimate from the charges made to individual customers.

In the detailed discussions which followed, the banks brought in the leasing specialists in their related finance houses, and in particular Victor Adey, Chairman of Mercantile Credit, who was to play a leading role in establishing and developing the leasing scheme. Negotiations also took place with the major car manufacturers and their dealer networks.

Although the banks would have the security of the automatic payment of individuals' mobility allowances to meet the cost of their leases – something unique in leasing schemes – they were nevertheless entering into a largely new field. They would have to take the risks of any adverse movements in the cost of money, VAT, corporation tax rates, inflation (which at that time was swinging up to and above 15 per cent), the rate of mobility allowance (which was not statutorily linked to the Retail Prices Index), administration expenses and all the other costs likely to be incurred. It was for this reason that the cost of leases had to include the contingency reserve explained later in this chapter. The hope was nevertheless that it would be possible to provide cars in return for leasing payments which would be met, in as many cases as possible, solely out of disabled people's mobility allowances.

In July 1978 Motability Finance Limited (MFL) was formed by the six major UK clearing Banks – the Bank of Scotland, Barclays, Lloyds, Midland, National Westminster and the Royal Bank of Scotland – with the objective of providing cars on lease for disabled people. Had the banks not agreed to set up this company, it is no exaggeration to say that Motability would never have existed, at any rate on the scale to which it has developed.

MFL's activities later extended to the hire purchase of new and used cars and powered wheelchairs, and to the supply of cars to war pensioners.

THE ARRANGEMENTS BETWEEN MOTABILITY AND MFL

Although dedicated to the provision of services to Motability, and administering the Schemes on Motability's behalf, MFL is owned by the banks, and is corporately and financially independent of Motability. At the outset it was staffed by men and women seconded – and in some cases permanently transferred – from the banks and their leasing subsidiaries, without whose expertise the operation might have run into serious difficulties or failed entirely. MFL's activities are covered by a service agreement with the charity, which includes the provision of regular information about its finances and agreement on the main parameters of its activities.

Motability requires MFL to give good value and good service to its disabled customers, and it monitors its financial performance by comparing its services with commercial firms, particularly in the contract hire and fleet hire business. The aim is to maintain all input prices at the lowest possible level.

The Schemes operated by MFL require the disabled person to commit his or her allowance either in whole or in part for the term of the underlying agreement in payment of the lease (now contract hire) rentals or hire purchase instalments. The payments are made direct to MFL by the Benefits Agency.

Accordingly, under the terms of the scheme MFL receives from the customer:

In the case of contract hire, an assignment for the period of the agreement of the higher rate mobility component of the disability living allowance (or war pensioners' supplement), and (normally) of any future uprating increases, and where this does not cover the total a lump sum by way of advance payment to make up the difference.

In the case of hire purchase, an assignment for the period of the agreement of the mobility component at the rate in force at the time of the agreement, plus an initial deposit.

CONTRACT HIRE

Payments to MFL by customers of the contract hire scheme cover the cost of the money provided by the banks (including their profit margin); the purchase price of the vehicles, their depreciation and maintenance; insurance of the vehicles; roadside assistance costs; a variable contingency margin; and MFL's administration costs and the banks' management fees.

The distribution of these costs can best be expressed in diagrammatic form. The following chart, taken with permission from the NAO Report discussed in Chapter 14, shows how the cost of a typical contract hire agreement is made up.

It will be seen from the chart that MFL itself is a non-profit-making company. The limited profits from the schemes are made by the banks in the provision of funds for MFL.

Breakdown of the total cost of a typical three-year contract hire agreement

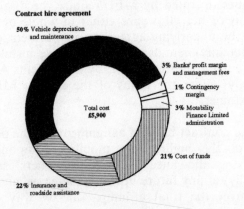

Contract hire agreement

50% Vehicle depreciation and maintenance

3% Banks' profit margin and management fees

1% Contingency margin

3% Motability Finance Limited administration

Total cost £5,900

21% Cost of funds

22% Insurance and roadside assistance

Notes:

1. *Costs are based upon a typical vehicle supplied through Motability's contract hire scheme in January 1996.*

2. *Vehicle depreciation is calculated from the purchase price of the vehicle less the guaranteed price paid by the manufacturer's agent, such as a car dealer, at the end of the contract.*

3. *The total cost of supplying a typical vehicle for a three year period is £5,900. These costs would be met by the user from their mobility benefit (over 156 weeks) plus an initial down payment of £453.*

THE COST OF THE MONEY PROVIDED BY THE BANKS

At the end of 1996 the banks' total commitment to the Motability Schemes was £1,500,000,000, of which just over 80 per cent was represented by loans and the balance by deferred corporation tax and reserves.

The banks borrow the money to finance the Motability Schemes from the money markets. The interest which they have to pay on the money borrowed, plus a margin which is renegotiated with Motability at regular intervals, is included in the leasing charge. The margin is variable, but it has been gradually reduced in recent years. In August 1995 Motability commissioned a merchant bank (Schroders) to examine the cost of finance as compared with market rates for similar lending, and following this review the margin was reduced to 1 per cent. In addition to this margin, each of the six banks receives management fees of £50,000 per annum.

Under the Capital Allowances Act, tax relief obtained through the acquisition of cars is beneficially passed to the customer in the calculation of the lease rental.

The financial returns to the banks are typified in the following figures for the year ended 30 September 1996.

	£000
Average value of loans	1,107,795
Gross margin earned	14,630
Management fees	300
Total profits before tax	14,930
Less: Corporation tax at 33 per cent	4,927
Profit after tax	10,003

The banks have been called upon to provide an ever-increasing supply of funds, and they have done this through times of recession and inflation. Throughout the history of MFL, they have in addition given valuable support to its management.

THE OVERALL COST OF VEHICLES

A manufacturer and its associated dealer network wishing to participate in the leasing scheme have to satisfy certain conditions as to their financial soundness and the service the dealer will offer to disabled customers. The dealers then enter into an agreement under which they agree to sell vehicles to MFL, to provide maintenance over the hiring period, and to buy the vehicle back at the end of the period, subject to its being in reasonable condition. The sale price, maintenance charges and residual value are negotiated with the vehicle manufacturers.

Certain manufacturers use centralised maintenance agents other than the supplying dealer to service the vehicle throughout the three-year contract hire period, and also undertake the buying-back obligation. In some cases, MFL itself arranges for vehicle maintenance.

The terms agreed with the manufacturers are negotiated by MFL and reviewed by Motability on a continuous basis. For the contract hire scheme, manufacturers tend to view the net sale price (less discounts), maintenance charges and buy-back prices as a whole, and it would therefore be misleading to focus on one aspect of the leasing package in isolation. When prices are being negotiated, MFL supplies manufacturers with details of the initial hire payment which would arise from the prices being suggested, and as a result manufacturers amend the mix of purchase discount, maintenance charges and buy-back price to fix an initial payment which they think will be competitive.

This competition between the manufacturers ensures that the prices include discounts which are substantially higher than are normally available, to the advantage of Motability's customers.

Fundamental changes in the present system, under which MFL would become wholly responsible for maintenance and residual values, are at present under consideration (see Chapter 14).

Insurance

MFL uniquely provides fully comprehensive insurance on a fleet basis for cars on contract hire, including loss of use cover and uninsured loss recovery. Premiums are recovered through the rental charges. The insurance arrangements are reviewed on a regular basis by MFL and Motability.

The contract hire fleet was insured from 1978 until 1989 with the Zurich Insurance Company, who rendered valuable service to the scheme. In 1989 insurance was taken over by Municipal Mutual Insurance (MMI), who provided a competitive fixed premium throughout the three years of an agreement.

The collapse of MMI in 1992 made it urgently necessary to seek another insurer, and the insurance of cars under contract hire was then transferred to Eagle Star, on a similar three-year arrangement. Users of cars on contract hire and insured with MMI were assured that they could continue to be used and that claims for their cars would be met. Special telephone enquiry lines were set up for this purpose.

Negotiations, in which Lord Sterling and Gerry Acher of Motability played a leading part, (and advice was received from Government Departments), were carried out with the parties concerned to ensure that no extra costs were borne by Motability Scheme users as a result of the transfer of commitments from MMI. In the event, losses which could have amounted to £20,000,000 were limited to under £1,000,000.

After three years of valuable service by Eagle Star, the insurance contract was renewed in 1995 with Royal Insurance (now Royal & Sun Alliance). A freephone telephone number for customers is available at the company's dedicated Motability facility in Liverpool (Royal & Sun Alliance 'Motability'), and Royal's staff are able to manage any incident or accident from the initial report and the provision (if necessary) of a replacement car to the return of the repaired car.

Reductions in insurance premiums and other cost savings

negotiated by MFL made it possible for the first time to provide some cars for a rental less than the full allowance, as described in Chapter 3.

Roadside assistance services

The roadside assistance services included in the leasing package were re-assessed by Motability and MFL in 1994, when a number of organisations were invited to tender. The contract was awarded to the Automobile Association, which created a special product for Motability customers, known as AA Motability Assistance, described in Chapter 3. In 1997 the contract was awarded to the RAC.

The contingency reserve

In fixing the price of leases, MFL aims to make neither a profit nor a loss. Some of the costs i.e. those dealt with above, can be determined in advance, but in accordance with good industry practice it has been necessary to provide a contingency margin, to create a reserve to guard against certain risks and so protect current and future customers. Among the factors which have to be taken into account and which may produce losses are the following:

Prevailing interest rates determined by reference to the global money markets and their effect on the cost of money to the banks
Changes in corporation tax and capital allowances
The amount of increase in the rates of the higher rate mobility component of the disability living allowance (and the war pensioner's supplement), which depend on the movement of the Retail Prices Index

MFL has to make assumptions about these factors, which cannot be altered once a contract has been signed.

There are other risks and uncertainties which have to be borne by the Scheme as a whole, for example, when a contract hire agreement does not run its full term e.g. because, for one of a number of reasons, a customer becomes disentitled to the allowance, or the agreement is prematurely terminated for bona fide reasons such as death or increased disability. Some 20 per cent of agreements do not run their full term.

In October 1997, for example, there were 1,552 early terminations – 48 per cent because of death or increased disability, 30 per cent because a different car was required before the end of the agreement, and 16 per cent because the disabled person was a passenger and a driver was no longer available.

In these circumstances the car is not bought back by the dealer, and it has to be sold to the best advantage in the secondhand car market prevailing at the time. As an example, in early 1993 vehicle sale losses amounted to £372 for each car sold, with losses on rejected or abused vehicles reaching £1,195 per vehicle. At present, conditions in the market are more favourable, but they are not obviously predictable, and could always change for the worse.

A further factor which is outside the control of MFL is the adverse impact on the Scheme of the financial collapse of a major motor dealer or maintenance agent. In such circumstances motor manufacturers' indemnities could be called upon to mitigate the loss, but the risk would be significant.

The reserve to provide for possible losses is set from time to time, as a percentage of the amount required to fund the leases, in consultation with Motability. Initially, the level of this margin was audited by the Department. However, since 1984 the examination has been carried out by independent auditors, and it is then used as the basis for discussion with Motability, in order to set the reserve required by MFL to cover any adverse movement in the evaluation factors mentioned above. In all these discussions the late Alan Outten, who was a member of the founding committee set up by the banks in 1977, and served on the Board of MFL until 1992, played a key role.

If the level of reserves set aside by MFL is sufficient over time to protect against all potential adverse movements in the assumptions made, any excess belongs to Motability and is available for the benefit of customers. For example, in 1994 favourable changes in the rate of corporation tax produced an unexpected surplus which enabled MFL, with Motability's agreement, to provide customers with a rebate of rentals, and in 1988 the benefit of a fall in interest rates was passed on to Motability in the form of a transfer of £5,000,000 to the newly-established Tenth Anniversary Trust Fund, which supplements Motability's charitable fund. This contribution was matched by a similar amount from the Government in the form of an interest-free loan. MFL has since made further transfers to Motability under a covenant from surpluses in the contingency reserve, making the total paid over up to March 1997 over £34,000,000. These contributions have in turn been transferred by Motability to the Tenth Anniversary Trust Fund.

The setting of the reserve involves a balance between what is financially prudent and the cost of contract hire to the customer. Although surpluses in the reserve are passed to Motability, it is important that the cost of contract hire should be kept to the minimum i.e. that the generality of customers should not in effect be contributing an excessive amount to the reserve from which they will not benefit directly.

In accordance with this principle, the contingency margin has been reduced progressively, in line with UK economic conditions, from one per cent in 1994 to 0.5 per cent from June 1995, and it was completely removed from April 1996. As a result, prospective prices were reduced from that date for all new customers, by approximately £80 over the three years of a typical contract hire agreement. This will have the effect of slowing down the accumulation of reserves as existing agreements expire. The surplus reserves held by MFL, £26,900,000 at the time, will therefore be used for the benefit of existing customers, including the two-thirds who typically renew their agreements.

Administration expenses

MFL's administration costs, amounting to £16,000,000 in the year to September 1996, represent the smallest of the inputs to the leasing charges – just 0.75 per cent of the cost of leases. Motability has been looking, with MFL, at the benchmarking of these costs to ensure value for money.

Hire purchase

The basis of the hire purchase schemes provided by MFL is set out in Chapter 3.

FINANCIAL EXAMINATION

Annual examinations of the financial aspects of MFL's operations have been prepared for Motability by Richard Bennison of KPMG, covering among other matters the cost of the money provided by the banks and the size of the contingency reserve. These have satisfied the Governors that good value is being provided for disabled customers, and they have led to the reductions in costs described above.

To provide further reassurance, the Schroders study referred to above confirmed the results of KPMG's reviews, as has the report of the National Audit Office (NAO) (see Chapter 14) which showed that MFL's contract hire rates are significantly lower, by an average of 30 per cent, than those charged by other contract hire companies to large fleet operators. The NAO Report also showed that services accounting for 70 per cent of the cost of the leasing scheme are obtained by competitive tender, the remaining 30 per cent being the cost of borrowing the money, the banks' margin and MFL's administration costs.

Motability has commissioned Schroders to produce a study of the possibility of introducing forms of competition in the provision of the services provided by MFL.

THE MANAGEMENT OF MFL

MFL's Board is made up of eight non-executive directors, including the Chairman, and drawn from each of the shareholder banks' subsidiaries, and three executive directors, including the Chief Executive. The Board, which meets at least four times a year, was chaired from 1977 to 1985 by Sir John Quinton, who has been a Governor of Motability since that time. From 1985 the chair was taken by Brian Goldthorpe, Deputy Chief Executive of the Midland Bank, who, until his untimely death in 1992, made an invaluable contribution not only to MFL but also to Motability, of which he became a Governor in 1987. His place was taken by Brian Carte, Chief Executive of Lombard North Central, who was also appointed as a Governor of Motability, and in June 1995 he was replaced by David Harrison, Director of Corporate and Institutional Banking of Lloyds Bank.

The Board decides overall business policy and the level of funding required by MFL. At least once a year it receives a detailed report which covers the business activities of the company, and in particular submits recommendations for funding levels and any other changes in policy.

Responsibility for the day-to-day management of MFL is vested in its Chief Executive, who is also an executive director of the MFL board. This position was first held by Harry Hall, and later by John Jackson. On his retirement early in 1987, he was replaced by Malcolm Titchener of Lloyds Bank. When he retired in 1992, his place was filled by Brian Hassell, who left in 1994 and was replaced by Ed Lester. MFL has been ably led by all these Chief Executives. Ed Lester in particular has successfully coped with the many changes required to meet the greatly increased volume of work.

Originally, as already mentioned, the staff of MFL was drawn from the shareholding banks. However, the changing nature of the company and the increasing demands for special-ist staff have led to the majority of the current staff, who number at present 280, being recruited direct from the market.

As explained above, although MFL and Motability are separate organisations, they work very closely together in the administration of the Scheme and in negotiations with the major motor manufacturers and dealers, the insurance

48

companies and the motoring organisations. Motability greatly values the contribution which the staff of MFL have made to the success of the enterprise.

5

TRIKE DRIVERS

As explained in Chapter 1, the trike preceded the mobility allowance as the Government provision for the mobility of severely disabled people. It was superseded by the allowance in 1976, but people issued with a trike before 1 January 1976 were given, and still have, the opportunity to transfer automatically to the mobility allowance (now the mobility component of disability living allowance) i.e. without a medical examination or limit on age. Other trike drivers had to apply in the normal way for the allowance.

Motability decided at the outset of its schemes, however, not to issue a general invitation to trike drivers to switch to the allowance and a Motability Scheme car, on the grounds that for the time being they had a satisfactory means of mobility and were in any case the responsibility of the Government. For the same reason, although some trike drivers transferred on their own initiative, it was initially decided not to use Motability's own charitable fund to supplement the allowance, even if it was not sufficient to obtain the car they wanted.

What is said here applies also to the relatively few people who had had a Government car instead of a trike under the previous scheme.

ASSISTANCE FROM THE DEPARTMENTS

In 1979 a report of a study of the needs of trike drivers, which had been commissioned from the Motor Industries Research Association by the Department, was published. It looked forward to a time when, for various reasons,

50

The first Motability Scheme vehicle, 1978.

Julie Newport, one of ten young people who attended the first Motability Scheme vehicle handover held at Earls Court London on 25 July 1978. She received the keys to her new vehicle from Chairman Lord Goodman (right). Also present is The Rt Hon Lord Morris (2nd left).

Schools were to the fore in fundraising activities during 1984. A 'Carolthon' took place at the Barbican attended by hundreds of London school children, hosted by TV celebrities Val Singleton and Nerys Hughes, seen here with orchestra members from Sladebrook School.

'Fund-A-Car' Kent ran during the autumn term of 1984, raising over £10,000, and enjoyed the support of the Archbishop of Canterbury, who hosted a vehicle handover with Clive Wilson, a Motability Scheme customer, at the Old Palace, Canterbury.

The first ever 'Fund-A-Car' ceremony. Considerable sums of money were raised by the Manchester schools participating, and Sir Hugh Rossi met some of the children at the prize-giving ceremony, 1985.

Mr Robert Wykes presenting a cheque on Motability's stand at Motorfair 1987 to Sir Peter Large CBE, Governor of Motability. Left to right are Lord Sterling, Allan Beard CB CBE and Sir Nicholas Scott.

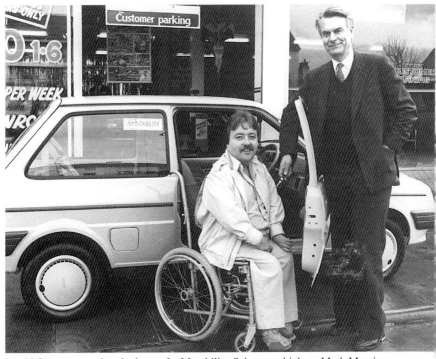

David Owen presenting the keys of a Motability Scheme vehicle to Mark May in Plymouth 1987.

Former Prime Minister The Rt Hon Baroness Thatcher handing over the key to a new Motability Scheme vehicle outside 10 Downing Street in April 1987.

The Rt Hon Neil Kinnock speaking at the Motorfair, 1989. From left to right Ken Keen, Director, Lord Sterling, Vice Chairman, Joe Hennessey OBE, Governor, Sir Peter Large CBE, Governor, Allan Beard CB CBE, Treasurer.

The Rt Hon Neil Kinnock, Patron of Motability, with an exhibitor at the Motability Lead-free campaign, Motorfair 1989.

Former Prime Minister The R Hon Baroness Thatcher handing over a new Motability Scheme vehicle to Carole Walters at 10 Downing Street a a ceremony to celebrate the 200,000th car supplied by the Motability Scheme, 1990.

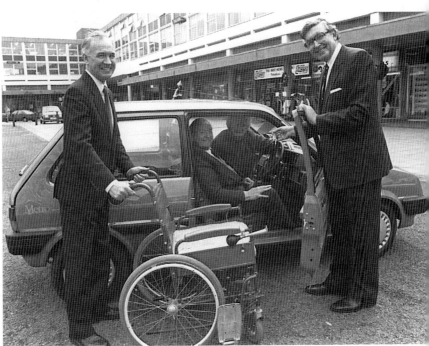

March 1991, The Rt Hon Lord Jenkin (right) hands keys of a new vehicle to Motabilit Scheme customer Ted Wallace.

remaining trike drivers could no longer be provided with a suitable trike, and assessed the extent to which they could then continue to be made mobile with a suitably adapted car, in accordance with the pledge given by the Government in 1976 (see Chapter 1). The conclusion of the study was that well over 90 per cent of the existing trike drivers could be accommodated in this way, and that the main problem would be access to the new vehicle rather than adaptations to the controls. There are now a number of ways in which this access can be provided for.

In 1980 the Government made funds available on a strictly limited basis to help drivers of trikes who wished to switch to the allowance and obtain a car through the Motability Scheme, but had insufficient resources for their particular needs. In 1982 this help was extended to the limited number of people who had cars instead of trikes under the old vehicle scheme. Finally, in 1987 the Government introduced arrangements whereby trike drivers who wished to buy used Departmental cars would be able to do so if surplus vehicles were available.

Government Departments made two special funds available for trike drivers, to be administered by Motability. One fund, of up to £100,000 a year, was provided by the Department of Health to be used solely to cover the provision of a standard, non-means-tested, package of adaptations to Motability Scheme cars acquired by people previously participating in the old vehicle scheme (principally trike drivers) described in Chapter 1. This included the initial payment for the contract hire of the least expensive suitable automatic vehicle available, and for a prescribed list of adaptations to controls, not including expensive items such as joystick steering or tailor-made power steering.

The second fund, of up to £50,000 a year, was provided by the Department of Social Security for grants, but only according to means, normally of up to £1,000 towards the advanced payment of a car where this was not covered by a grant from the first fund. Grants were also to be made from this fund for driving lessons. Where assessment is necessary, payment of the cost is made by the Department to the Mobility Centre.

These arrangements were notified to all remaining trike drivers and Government car users under the vehicle scheme. As a result of these schemes, deaths of drivers and other changes, the number of trikes on issue in the UK had declined to under 1,000 by July 1997, compared with over 21,000 in 1976.

Amounts provided by the Department

The amounts provided to Motability in recent years for the assistance of trike drivers under the arrangements described above are as follows:

	£
1989–90	80,558
1990–91	101,756
1991–92	127,459
1992–93	166,159
1993–94	170,893
1994–95	148,342
1995–96	93,914
1996–97	47,585
1997–98	62,654

The Mobility Equipment and Drivers Funds

In certain circumstances, awards to trike users from the Departmental funds may be topped up by supplementary grants from Motability's charitable fund. The provision by the Government of the Mobility Equipment and Drivers Funds (see Chapter 8) has also enabled Motability to consider the award of grants to Government vehicle users wishing to convert to Motability Scheme cars, whose financial requirements are not met by the two Departmental funds described above. There are not many of these cases, but they are costly. In view of the promise originally made to trike drivers, Motability would accordingly have preferred the Government to have made specific provision for those trike drivers who wish to transfer to other vehicles at substantial costs not met by the standard arrangements.

6

WAR PENSIONERS

In November 1983 a new mobility supplement to Government payments to war pensioners was introduced in place of the provision of Government cars, on broadly the same physical conditions as for what was then the civilian mobility allowance. Like that allowance, this gave a means of mobility which was available for the first time for passengers as well as drivers – previously the Department had provided cars for drivers only. Before the introduction of the supplement, Motability suggested to the Department and organisations representing war disabled people that pensioners who so wished should be able to use the new supplement in order to participate in Motability's existing contract hire and hire purchase schemes for civilian allowance recipients. This suggestion was accepted.

The great majority of the cars supplied in this way have been obtained on contract hire. At the end of June 1997, 6,455 war pensioners out of a total of just over 22,000 with the mobility supplement had agreements with MFL.

ASSISTANCE FROM THE DEPARTMENT

The war pensioners' mobility supplement (£38.55 a week at January 1998) is at a higher rate than the civilian allowance. It thus usually enables a war pensioner, if necessary, to obtain without further assistance a more expensive car (including adaptations) than a civilian allowance recipient unsupported

53

by other resources or a Motability grant. However, pensioners wishing to use the Motability Scheme who exceptionally need a car and adaptations which cannot be funded by their mobility supplement can receive assistance from funds made available by the Department. These funds are administered by Motability.

Subject to medical history, a number of non-means-tested standard allowances are available, covering automatic transmission, factory-fitted power steering (if this is an optional extra provided by the manufacturer), left-foot accelerator and hand controls to brakes and accelerator. Some other adaptations can be provided for; in practice, this is limited to two standard allowances. There is no budget for these grants, but they are made according to strict criteria laid down by the Department. In certain circumstances the Government grants may be topped up by grants from Motability's charitable fund or from the Mobility Equipment or Drivers Funds described in Chapter 8.

In the year ended March 1997, 895 grants were made from the Funds provided by the Department.

Under the Department's scheme of funding for adaptations, automatic transmission was at first authorised only for left-leg amputees. Motability pointed out, however, that in dealing with comparable civilian cases applying for a charitable grant it had always taken the view, on grounds of safety, that both right and left leg amputees need an automatic gearbox. As a result of these representations, the Department agreed in 1987 to come into line with Motability's practice. This change was greatly welcomed by the British Limbless Ex-Servicemen's Association.

The arrangements made by the Department also enabled pensioner drivers using the cars which it had previously provided, to buy them for a lump sum at preferential prices, if necessary through Motability's used car hire purchase scheme.

In 1985 the Department agreed to meet the cost of adapting replacement cars needed where leases were prematurely terminated because the war pensioner's increasing disability made the previously hired car unsuitable.

Amounts provided by the Department

The amounts provided in recent years to Motability for the assistance of war pensioners under the arrangements described above are as follows:

	£
1989–90	105,498
1990–91	197,077
1991–92	208,594
1992–93	232,589
1993–94	365,878
1994–95	400,078
1995–96	315,389
1996–97	271,654
1997–98	220,053

REPRESENTATION OF WAR PENSIONERS

When war pensioners were brought into the Scheme, Philip Dixon of the British Legion was appointed as a member of Motability. From 1984 Brian Fox of BLESMA attended meetings of the Executive Committee, and in 1987 he became a Governor. He gave up these offices on leaving BLESMA in 1989.

7

FINDING OUT WHAT CUSTOMERS THINK

It has always been important for Motability to find out what users think of the services provided and to take account of their views in the continuing work of improving its schemes.

Two major surveys of customers were carried out for this purpose in 1984 and 1993, providing a wealth of information about the characteristics of customers, the vehicles they chose, what they thought about them, and their degree of satisfaction with the different components of the schemes.

The 1984 survey covered the whole range of services i.e. the car hire and the car and wheelchair hire purchase schemes, and it questioned potential, current and past users. Professor Louis Moss, formerly Head of the Government Social Survey, carried out the initial design of the project and acted as consultant for the rest of the planning. The final design of the study and its execution were undertaken by Professor Gerald Hoinville, who wrote the report. The 1993 survey was commissioned by the Customer Affairs Committee and designed by Dr Wendy Sykes, who wrote the report. It concentrated on current car hire customers.

For both surveys data processing, computing and the statistical analyses were produced by Dr Peter Taylor of the University of the West of England. The results of the two surveys are summarised in Appendix 10.

The 1984 survey

The 1984 survey showed that the majority of customers were satisfied with their cars – 67 per cent were very satisfied. It pointed, however, to the need for improvements in Motability's services, and these were the subject of further study. The main need disclosed was for an improvement in the quality of the introductory leaflet and the booklets on new cars, used cars and electric wheelchairs. A complete revision of these publications in the light of the points raised in the survey was therefore undertaken. Motability is indebted to Roly Stafford, who was largely responsible for bringing about a transformation in the material. The new literature set out the information in a much clearer and more attractive manner, illustrated by photographs.

The survey report emphasised the financial problems of the majority of mobility allowance recipients, the effect this has on their attitude to Motability's schemes, and the question of financial help. Since then, the removal of car tax on contract hire cars has made it a good deal easier to acquire a Motability Scheme car, and the establishment of the Tenth Anniversary Trust Fund and further help from the Government have made more grants possible.

Apart from the removal of car tax already referred to, there have been improvements since the survey in the insurance terms for contract hire cars, including full roadside cover and off-the-road insurance. The computerised system of handling applications has greatly reduced the time people have to wait for a car. Many dealers have improved their service and their maintenance arrangements, and the Code of Practice developed by the Technical Committee brought about further improvements.

The survey report made a number of references to the apparent need for counselling, either in regard to the choice of car or, more basically, to the possibility of becoming mobile. Motability set up a pilot scheme in Newcastle to look into these needs, but the results did not bear out a demand for such a service.

There was evidence in the survey of people buying unsuitable wheelchairs. The Technical Committee later prepared a leaflet, devised by Morigue Cornwell, giving practical advice on choosing a wheelchair, which is now sent by Motability to all

57

applicants for these vehicles. The Technical Committee also monitored complaints about wheelchairs supplied by Motability.

The 1993 survey

The 1993 survey confirmed the general satisfaction of customers with the car hire scheme, but as will be seen from Appendix 10, it was clear that in spite of the changes made after the previous survey, improvements were still needed. These included a raising of the standards in the insurance contract.

A key element was again the need for fuller information. As a result, the pamphlet about car hire was redesigned, and a periodical magazine, *Lifestyle*, was introduced to provide information for customers on a comprehensive basis and in a more informal way. Improvements were also made in the handling of telephone enquiries, and, most important of all, an ambitious programme of improvements across the whole range of Motability's services – Customer First – has since been introduced, as described in Chapter 15.

THE CUSTOMER SATISFACTION SURVEY

Studies like those described above can give valuable evidence of the scope for improvement, but they of necessity do so at fairly long intervals. In 1996 a change was made with the commissioning of an ongoing Customer Satisfaction Survey, which has the advantage of a regular recording on a consistent basis of the opinions of customers, so enabling a close watch to be kept on trends.

The object of this newly-introduced survey, which is part of the Customer First Initiative, is, like that of the earlier surveys, to gain a better understanding of customers' views and attitudes towards the service and to look at ways in which this could be improved. The survey is undertaken by an independent market research company, part of the NOP Research Group.

As a preliminary step, a qualitative survey was carried out, involving a number of face-to-face interviews with Motability Scheme users. This enabled the company to develop a questionnaire which is being sent on a regular basis to a larger sample of customers. The results of these surveys, which are expected to cover more than 12,000 customers a year, are continuously monitored and made available to other interested bodies and publications.

The first quarterly survey, producing 2,585 customer replies, covered a very wide range of all aspects of the car hire scheme and its users, including:

Age and marital status
Processing of the disability allowance
How customers became aware of the Scheme
Previous transport
Car choice and suitability of the car
Adaptations
Experience with Motability
Experience with MFL
Experience with other service providers
Choice of dealer
Degree of satisfaction with the dealer
Repair and servicing arrangements
Additional services e.g. courtesy car
Readership of *Lifestyle* magazine

The characteristics found in customers e.g. age distribution and working status, corresponded closely with those found in the earlier surveys. The results of the first of the regular surveys are at present being analysed, but they provide encouraging evidence of the beneficial effect of the improvements in customer service made since 1995.

8

THE TENTH ANNIVERSARY TRUST FUND AND THE MOBILITY EQUIPMENT AND DRIVERS FUNDS

THE TENTH ANNIVERSARY TRUST FUND

By 1988 it had become clear that Motability's charitable fund would not be sufficient to meet the growing demand for grants to disabled people who wished to achieve personal mobility for the first time, and to assure continued mobility for those who wanted a new car at the end of their contract hire agreement. Further support was needed, and fortunately it became available in the form of a surplus of £5,000,000 in MFL's contingency reserve which accrued to the credit of Motability. This was matched by a similar sum from the Government, and these two payments made possible the creation of a new special trust fund to support Motability's charitable fund.

The establishment of this fund, to be called the Tenth Anniversary Trust Fund to mark ten years of Motability's services, was announced in the House of Commons on 27 October 1988 by the Minister for Disabled People, The Rt Hon Sir Nicholas Scott. A trust, to be called the Motability Tenth Anniversary Trust, was set up on 16 March 1989 to administer the Fund. It was established as a charitable company limited by guarantee, with the late Lord Goodman as the founding Chairman of the Board of Trustees.

The general object of the Trust, as stated in its memorandum of association, is 'to facilitate the relief and assistance of disabled persons...in connection with the provision to the beneficiaries of personal or other transportation by assisting, promoting and supporting Motability'. Particular objects include the promotion and encouragement of research and investigation into and experiments in the manufacture, modification, use and maintenance of motor vehicles. An example of this is the grant made to pay for a study by Cranfield University, commissioned by Motability, into the market for a small vehicle for wheelchair drivers (see Chapter 13).

Under the articles of association, the Secretary of State for Social Security has the right to appoint a maximum of two Trustees, MFL a maximum of two, and Motability a maximum of three. The Secretary of State's appointees are Derek Chislett and Sir Peter Large; MFL's are Brian Carte and Alan Moore; and Motability's are Gerald Acher, Allan Beard and Sir John Quinton. Lord Sterling is the Chairman, and Sir John the Vice-Chairman.

The finances of the Fund

Motability has continued to transfer the surpluses received from MFL's contingency fund to the Tenth Anniversary Trust Fund. Up to the end of the financial year 1996–97 the total transferred in this way was £34,311,000. The money has been invested by merchant bankers appointed by the Trustees. As explained in Chapter 4, from 1996 the contingency reserve was removed, so that payments from this source were discontinued.

The policy of the Trustees has so far been to preserve and enhance the real value of the original endowment, using only the income produced by investment for assistance to Motability. The payments made in this way have been as follows:

	£
1990–91	733,567
1991–92	1,794,655
1992–93	2,006,936
1993–94	2,699,968
1994–95	1,300,000
1995–96	1,528,934
1996–97	350,000
1997–98	1,404,000

Projections are regularly made by Motability of the future demands likely to be made on the Tenth Anniversary Trust Fund to supplement Motability's charitable fund, taking account of the expected increasing need for help in renewal cases. In September 1997 it was estimated that the annual requirement could rise to over £3,000,000 in the year 2001–2002.

In February 1997 the Trustees decided to make £1,000,000 available to assist the Mobility Equipment Fund (MEF), which is dealt with below.

The accumulated value of the Fund had risen by 31 March 1997 to £55,325,909, and the Trustees were able to consider whether it would be possible to make further disbursements for the purposes for which the Fund had been established. In doing so, they had to bear in mind that the prevailing economic factors favourable to low costs for Motability Scheme cars – low inflation and oversupply in the car industry – which had brought about a reduction in the demands on the charitable fund, might well not continue, with a consequent increase in the volume and amount of grants. Above all, it was essential to ensure that money would be available to meet the need for grants in the growing number of renewal cases.

After taking account of these factors, the Trustees decided in June 1997, at the request of Motability, to provide a grant which would enable Motability to make substantial easements in the financial conditions for grants from the charitable fund, the MEF and the Drivers Funds; and to provide some additional assistance outside the present rules. These changes were estimated to cost up to £1,000,000.

In addition, it was decided to provide £100,000 for research, £300,000 to assist assessments at mobility centres, £100,000 for a Motability assessment vehicle, and £100,000 for the Equal Mobility project described in Chapter 13.

THE MOBILITY EQUIPMENT FUND AND THE DRIVERS FUND

In his original announcement about the Tenth Anniversary Trust Fund the Minister said that 'the new fund would increase five-fold the money available for Motability to spend each year, and in particular would in future provide extra help for the more severely disabled people who need a specially adapted vehicle'. An increase in grants of this order was indeed made possible between 1988 and 1991, and out of the total granted in 1990–91 Motability was able to provide £100,000 for the particular group envisaged by the Minister. But the extra resources from the Fund had in the event to be used mainly to supplement payments from Motability's own funds for the renewal of contract hire agreements in existing cases, which has always been regarded as the first priority in making grants, rather than for specially expensive new cases.

For the reasons given above, it was apparent that, even with the help of the Tenth Anniversary Trust Fund and an increase in the funds raised directly by Motability, there would be insufficient resources to help all the more severely disabled people needing particularly large grants. In April 1989 the Banstead Mobility Centre carried out a survey of the mobility status and equipment requirements of 1,000 mobility allowance recipients. This provided evidence for a request to the Government for additional help made by a consortium of disabled people's organisations, led by Queen Elizabeth's Foundation for the Disabled. Morigue Cornwell MBE of the Banstead Centre took a leading part in these developments.

These representations were successful, and as a result the Minister for Disabled People announced that the Government would provide £1,000,000 a year for three years, beginning in April 1991, specifically for people needing the most expensive vehicles or adaptations.

This money constitutes the Mobility Equipment Fund (MEF), which is administered by Motability on behalf of the Department. Regular detailed reports on the administration of the Fund (and of the Drivers Fund described below) are made by Motability to a review committee, which includes representatives of the Department and the charities concerned. The way in which the responsibility for cases is divided between Motability's own fund and the two special funds is explained in Chapter 9.

Before the payment of the first instalment of the Fund for 1991–92, Motability decided to allocate £150,000 from its own funds for use in the second half of 1990 for the kinds of cases intended to be covered by the Fund.

In 1992 the Minister for Disabled People announced that the Government had decided to continue its grant to the Fund for a further three years from April 1994, and to increase it from £1,000,000 to £2,000,000.

In 1993, as a result of representations led by the Spinal Injuries Association, the Minister promised that an additional £1,000,000 a year for three years, beginning in April 1994, would be made available to assist drivers who have to enter and/or drive their vehicle in a wheelchair. This became known as the Drivers Fund.

The consortium which first approached the Government was especially grateful for this continued support at a time of constraint in Government expenditure. The new funding has made it possible to increase the rate of grant giving, although it has been thought prudent, with the agreement of the Department and the other charities concerned, to continue the restrictions on individual grants explained in Chapter 9, where the principles and procedures for grants are explained. Chapter 9 also gives figures for the grants made from the two Funds.

The Department of Social Security is at present carrying out a comprehensive review of the operation of the MEF and Drivers Funds. In the meantime grants to the two Funds have continued on an annual basis.

9

SUPPLEMENTING THE MOBILITY ALLOWANCE: GRANTS FOR CARS

When Motability was first set up in 1977, it was recognised by the Government and all the parties concerned that there would be some disabled people who had insufficient resources of their own, apart from the mobility allowance, to use the Motability Scheme, in spite of the advantageous terms provided. From the start of its operations, Motability therefore began to raise funds for grants to such people. Without these grants for the advance payment for a car and the cost of any adaptations required, many people would have been unable to achieve personal mobility.

Originally, the only source of funds for grants was Motability's own charitable fund. This was supplemented from 1988 by the Tenth Anniversary Trust Fund. The charitable fund was not, however, able to provide for people with exceptionally severe disabilities who needed an expensive vehicle and/or adaptations. These people have since been able to receive grants from the two special Funds provided by the Department – the Mobility Equipment Fund (MEF) from 1991, and the Drivers Fund from 1994. In addition, there are two separate special Government funds to assist trike drivers and war pensioners to obtain Motability Scheme cars, described in Chapters 5 and 6 respectively.

The total of grants made by Motability from all these sources in 1996–97 was £4,250,115, a figure which demonstrates the heavy responsibilities borne by the grants staff.

CONDITIONS FOR THE MAKING OF GRANTS

What is said here applies in general, whatever the source of the grant. Conditions applying to particular kinds of grants are dealt with in the appropriate sections below.

Grants are made for driving lessons, but Motability is unable to help with running costs. Where, as in the majority of cases, the customer has chosen contract hire as the means of obtaining a car, these costs of course virtually amount only to the purchase of petrol. Indeed, in certain cases, as explained in Chapter 3, less than the full allowance is required for the rental, and the balance is available for running expenses.

Contributions by applicants

Motability's policy in grant making has always been to encourage self-help by disabled people, and, because of the demands on funds, to limit the provision made to the least expensive suitable car and adaptations available, provided always that this would meet their basic mobility requirements. For these reasons, applicants are asked where appropriate to consider whether a less expensive vehicle than they would ideally like to have would suffice.

Occasionally, applicants will ask to be allowed to 'top up' a grant from their own resources, to enable them to obtain a more expensive car than the one for which a grant has been offered. It has always been Motability's policy to decline such proposals, on the grounds that the extra resources available for 'topping up' could be used to reduce the amount of the grant required for what is judged to be a suitable vehicle.

In the early years of Motability, its own fund was sufficient to meet the need for all but the most expensive grants. In 1986, however, the increasing calls on the fund made it necessary to apply restrictions in cases where people were applying for a car for the first time – a limit of £1,000 to individual grants and a requirement to contribute the equivalent of eight weeks' allowance in advance towards the cost of the car. Help from the Tenth Anniversary Trust Fund made it possible in 1988 to do away with the individual grant limit, but the contribution requirement was maintained.

Early in 1992, it was realised that the ever-increasing demand would again soon outstrip the available funds unless there were further restrictions. The lump sum contribution in new cases was therefore increased to 16 weeks' allowance (about £480 at the rate in November 1992), and a contribution of £150 was asked for for the first time from all applicants wishing to renew their contract hire agreement, unless there were special circumstances. These contributions were later increased to £500 in new cases and £250 in renewal cases, subject again to waiving in special circumstances.

In 1997 a grant from the Tenth Anniversary Trust Fund enabled Motability to reduce the customer contribution to £300 in new cases and to £150 in renewal cases, and a number of other easements were introduced. Savings of more than £3,000 and any disposable income may also be taken into account, although this applies to only a few cases.

In the case of a grant for hire purchase, the applicant is required to sign an agreement protecting Motability's part of the investment if the agreement is terminated for any reason.

Considering the very high proportion of Motability's customers who are dependent on Social Security benefits – see the report of the Motability surveys in Appendix 10 – it is a tribute to the success of the Motability Schemes in keeping down the cost of acquiring a car, and to the readiness of disabled people to make sacrifices in order to do so, that the number needing a grant, although large, is not higher.

Contributions from other sources

Wherever possible, Motability hopes that other grant-giving charities set up to help people with particular disabilities will make a contribution towards the sum needed by applicants with those disabilities. In appropriate cases applicants are therefore asked to consider an approach to another charity, the names and addresses of suitable charities being provided. The award of a grant is not, however, made conditional upon such help.

In certain cases of people in work, the Employment Service is able to give some assistance with the cost of necessary adaptations.

Waiting lists

In general, applications for grants, whatever the fund, are dealt with in order of receipt, but this means, given the limited availability of funds, that applicants may have to be placed on a waiting list, which may involve a delay of some months. Priority is, however, given where possible to cases of urgent need, including those where a change in circumstances necessitates the early termination of an agreement and the urgent provision of a different vehicle. At the present time there is no waiting list for grants from Motability's own fund, although one has been necessary in the past, and it may have to be reinstated.

This waiting period has enabled some applicants to reduce their requirements or find other resources in the time available, and so to manage with a smaller grant, or sometimes without a grant at all.

GRANTS FROM MOTABILITY'S CHARITABLE FUND

There are many vehicles available on contract hire with a low advance payment, and others with no advance payment at all. Some customers, however, need larger vehicles, sometimes with automatic transmission or power-assisted steering, which require an advance rental beyond their means. The charitable fund is able to assist with this payment, and is also able to pay for certain combinations of simple adaptations. The upper limits of grants payable from the charitable fund are set by the lower limits of the MEF, which are detailed below.

Grants can be made for the cost of adaptations, above the first £300, to non-Motability vehicles owned by disabled people with the Government allowance. (An AA inspection is

68

required if the adaptations are to a vehicle which is over five years old and has covered more than 60,000 miles; if they are non-transferable; and their cost exceeds 50 per cent of the value of the vehicle.) An additional condition is that the adaptations must cost less than a suitably adapted new vehicle. All applicants for such grants must have an allowance award of at least six months at the time when their application is received.

Grants are made for both passengers and drivers. Where the disabled person is a child in a large family, or an adult with more than three children, a large 'people-carrying' vehicle may be required.

When a contract hire agreement is approaching expiry, the aim of Motability is to arrange for the new contract, if it is required, to follow on the old one without interruption, so as to ensure that there is no loss of mobility. Customers are therefore sent a package of information about six months before the end of the contract, inviting them to think about their new car and explaining how to go about ordering it. The package includes information about grants, setting out the conditions described above. Failure by the customer to respond to this invitation may well jeopardise continued mobility.

The number of applications for charitable grants has steadily decreased since 1995. This is because of the improved terms on which cars can be supplied on contract hire. Thus there are currently about 100 vehicles available without an advanced payment. In addition, many vehicles can be supplied on the basis of a constant rental throughout the term of the agreement, permitting the return of the balance of the allowance on each uprating. The number of customers who need a grant has therefore steadily fallen.

In September 1997 it was estimated that the total demand on the charitable fund could rise to over £4,000,000 in the year 2001. If present trends are maintained, this estimate may prove to be too high, but on the other hand, changes in economic circumstances may well have an adverse effect on the terms on which cars can be supplied, and so on expenditure from the fund.

Statistics of grants from the charitable fund

The annual totals of grants made from the charitable fund, which have grown from £41,695 in 1978–79 to £2,958,311 in 1997–98, are given in Appendix 3. The 1997–98 figure represented 5,289 grants. The growth in recent years is illustrated by the graph below.

Grants paid from the Motability Charitable Fund 1989 - 98

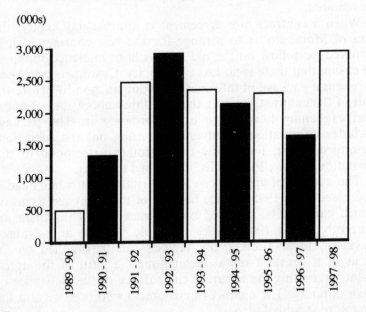

An analysis of 1996–97 expenditure is shown in the following two charts. Renewal customers represented 87 per cent of the total.

Special bulk purchasing from Nissan for grants cases, first introduced in 1993 to provide a small automatic car, has proved very successful. As a result there was a lower expendi-

Pattern of grants from the Charitable Fund 1997 - 98

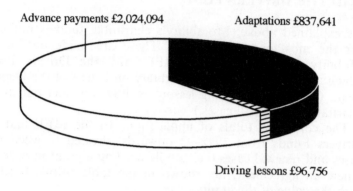

Advance payments £2,024,094

Adaptations £837,641

Driving lessons £96,756

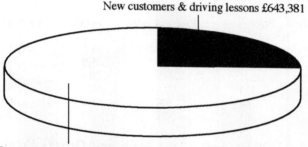

New customers & driving lessons £643,381

Renewal customers £2,314,930

ture on grants from 1993–94 onwards, as is illustrated in the chart. In 1995–96, for example, this special deal met the requirements of 1,700 customers, saving the fund over £1,000,000.

The lower prices that Motability was able to offer from October 1995 had a marked effect on the nature and extent of the demand for grants. Previously, the majority of applications were from people who needed a small-to-medium family car with a modest advance payment. From October 1995 onwards the reduction in advance payments made grants unnecessary in many of these cases, but there was a contrary effect because of an increase in the amount of grants, including those for 'people-carrying' vehicles.

71

GRANTS FROM THE MOBILITY EQUIPMENT FUND AND THE DRIVERS FUND

As explained above, Motability's charitable fund is not used for the most expensive grants. These are made out of the Mobility Equipment Fund (MEF) and the Drivers Fund, which are administered by Motability on behalf of the Department. (The cost of driving lessons is, however, met out of the charitable fund in all cases.)

The combined totals of applications to the MEF and the Drivers Funds from 1992–93 onwards, divided between new cases and renewal cases (i.e. people needing a grant in order to renew an agreement) are shown in the table below, together with the value of the grants.

	New cases	Renewal cases	Total	Value of grants £
1992–93	363	90	453	1,165,934
1993–94	243	282	525	1,792,357
1994–95	247	446	703	3,683,259
1995–96	229	324	553	2,142,075
1996–97	160	348	508	2,307,732
1997–98	203	528	731	4,456,636

In 1996–97, 20 per cent of the MEF and Drivers Fund applications were by drivers and 80 per cent by passengers. Over two-thirds were from people suffering from cerebral palsy (30 per cent), spinal cord diseases, genetic disorders or spinal injuries.

The administration of the two Funds, particularly the Drivers Fund, has proved complicated because of a number of interrelated factors. The amount actually expended each year must be kept within the limits of the Departmental allocation, subject to the very limited carry-over allowed by Treasury rules*, so that a shortfall in expenditure in an effort to avoid

* Exceptionally, the Treasury allowed the £300,000 shortfall in 1996–97 to be carried over into the next financial year.

exceeding the allocation could result in an irrecoverable loss of funds. The difficulty is compounded by the length of time needed to purchase and adapt the required vehicle and to make sure that it meets the needs of the customer, which causes uncertainty about the actual financial year in which the vehicle will have to be paid for. Added to these factors is the necessity for a waiting period mentioned above. This currently stands at up to 24 months. When the time elapsing before an application can come up for consideration is added to the lead time needed to supply the vehicle after a decision has been made to make a grant, there is inevitably a considerable delay.

For these reasons, the figures given on page 72 are for grants awarded during each year, and do not represent the actual amounts paid out in grants in the same periods. For example, a limitation in the amount of Drivers Fund grants in 1995–96 was necessitated by the large total of grants awarded, but not paid, in the previous year.

An investigation is being made into the possibility of devising an economical insurance package for the benefit of MEF and Drivers Fund customers who, because of the extent of their disability, need a heavily adapted vehicle which can only be provided under the hire purchase scheme, and which will often attract a high insurance premium.

In Chapter 10 there is an account of surveys of customers who had received a grant from the MEF or Drivers Fund. This was undertaken to find out whether the vehicles and adaptations provided had turned out to be the most suitable.

Recent improvements in procedure include a written appeals system and leaflets giving information on the schemes. A new computer system has been set up to facilitate the tracking of individual projects, the strategic planning of commitments, and the identification of more suitable adaptations to meet individual requirements.

THE MEF

The MEF is used to assist drivers needing grants above the charitable fund limits but not coming within the Drivers Fund categories (see below), all passengers needing grants for adaptations above the charitable fund limits, and passengers travelling in their wheelchair in specially converted rear-access vehicles.

The majority of grants are in fact for passengers, usually for rear-access vehicles. Grants above £10,000 are not normally needed in these cases, but in exceptional circumstances this figure may be exceeded.

The following cases are covered:

Advance payments for vehicles which are to have adaptations fitted which fall outside charitable fund limits.

Advance payments for rear-access vehicles, where the passenger enters and travels in a wheelchair.

Vehicles in exceptional circumstances for trike drivers, but only to the extent to which their need is not covered by the special Departmental fund for these drivers described in Chapter 5.

These rules are regularly reviewed according to the condition of the various funds.

Because of the high cost of the vehicles provided, the proper administration of the MEF requires as far as possible that repeated grants to the same person i.e. at the end of three year hire agreements, should be avoided. For this reason, a grant to assist hire purchase is considered in appropriate cases. Hire purchase makes the customer responsible for insurance and maintenance, which not all customers can afford, but it is possible to bring it within the means of some people if they are required to give up only a part of their allowance. This procedure calls for a larger initial grant, but no renewal grant, at any rate for a lengthy period.

Applications for MEF grants are now rising. The MEF is intended to assist those with the most severe disabilities, and many of the renewal applications, which constitute the majority of applications, are from people with increasing disabilities who previously obtained their Motability vehicle without the need for a grant or with a grant which could be made from the charitable fund. As mentioned in the previous chapter, £1,000,000 has been allocated from the Tenth Anniversary Trust Fund to deal with the increasing demand and to prevent the waiting list from first-time applicants from growing; and to cope with the reclassification of Drivers Fund cases mentioned below.

THE DRIVERS FUND

The Drivers Fund provides for drivers needing grants of more than £10,000 for vehicles and especially expensive equipment, in the following categories:

People who must remain seated in their wheelchair while driving, or who, while able to drive from a vehicle seat, need to enter the vehicle in a wheelchair.
Drivers, whether or not driving from a wheelchair, who need special steering controls, i.e:
Remote hydraulic two-way steering
Four-way joystick control
Electronic joystick
Horizontal or zero-effort steering
Tiller control

These vehicles and equipment can only be provided on hire purchase.

Until the availability of the Drivers Fund in April 1994 a normal limit of £10,000 had to be imposed on MEF grants, which meant that drivers needing especially expensive vehicles and adaptations were obliged to try to raise funds to supplement the grant in order to become mobile. As soon as the new Drivers Fund was announced a special review was made of these cases, with a new assessment where necessary, and the grants were immediately increased to the full amount required.

Originally, applications were dealt with on a first come, first served basis, and the emphasis was placed on providing independent driving for each applicant, regardless of family circumstances or the use to which the prospective vehicle would be put. This led to a large number of applications – 137 in the 18 months up to January 1996 – and to a waiting period between application and delivery of the vehicle which represented four years' funding. This was because during 1995–96, the second year of the availability of the Fund, grant applications had reached such a level that the waiting list had to be put on hold, no new applications being accepted, and efforts being concentrated on the projects already begun in 1994–95.

A further difficulty was that these projects were often found to require more extensive and expensive adaptation than had been originally estimated, and that they frequently required additional rectification work because of the relative inexperience of all concerned in this field.

The very long delays were clearly unacceptable, and given the inability of the Government to increase the amount of the Drivers Fund, it was essential to ensure that the limited funds were directed towards the people with the greatest need. It was therefore decided to carry out a review of all the 137 cases still waiting for a grant, based on a questionnaire to the applicants. It was clear that this was going to be a difficult exercise, which could well cause distress to applicants, and the questionnaire was therefore circulated in advance to all interested third parties, including mobility centres, disability groups and those MPs, social workers and other professional individuals who had taken up particular cases with Motability.

The results of this review have been studied to see whether in some cases earlier mobility could be achieved at a reduced cost – for example, where driving from a wheelchair is not absolutely essential, or travelling as a passenger in a suitable vehicle, given the availability of a driver, could be contemplated.

The reclassification of cases arising from this review has resulted in greater calls on the MEF, towards which assistance has been provided by the Tenth Anniversary Trust Fund. At the same time there has been a reduction in applications, because the review effectively meant that the Drivers Fund was closed for the time being.

The average grant at the present time is £24,000. This demonstrates how expensive these cases can be, and how important is the search for more economical transport. In the longer term, it is hoped that a study of the possible commercial development of a purpose-built rear-access vehicle for drivers (see Chapter 13) will bear fruit.

THE PROCEDURES FOR HANDLING GRANT APPLICATIONS

Originally, grants cases were mainly dealt with by the Executive Committee, but by 1990 they had become so numerous that it was decided to set up a Grants Committee to deal with them. This Committee authorised the larger grants from Motability's own fund, the remainder (the great majority) being handled by the staff at Harlow. The Committee later dealt in addition with all applications for grants from the MEF and the Drivers Fund.

The workload became so heavy, however, that in order to ensure proper consideration of applications it was decided in 1995 to delegate cases previously settled by the full Grants Committee to an in-house committee of the senior grants staff at Harlow, with Grants Committee members taking it in turn to chair the meetings. Before this change was made, a detailed statement of the principles to be applied by the staff and the new committee in dealing with grants applications was approved by the Grants Committee. Recently, further delegation in specified cases to the grants staff has been agreed.

The full Grants Committee still meets regularly to consider questions of principle and all appeals against grants decisions, and to deal with all requests for assistance from the Drivers Fund. Its members also take it in turns to carry out a sample check of the cases dealt with outside the in-house committee.

The Committee's members since its formation in 1990 have been Allan Beard (Chairman) and the three disabled Motability Governors – Joe Hennessy, Sir Peter Large and

Professor Adrian Stokes. Roly Stafford served as a member from 1990 until 1991. Allan Beard retired from the Committee in 1995, when Joe Hennessy took over the Chairmanship, and Sam Gallop OBE was appointed as a member. The current members, particularly the Chairman, bear a heavy load of work.

Management staff

For many years Robin Taylor was responsible for the administration of grants in addition to his other duties, but the rapid expansion in the work made it necessary to create a special post for the purpose. This was filled for some years by Mike Quinn.

In January 1996 responsibility passed to Mike Richards, who came to Motability from the Army with extensive experience of motor vehicles. He was appointed to the new post of Grants and Technical Director, and rapidly set up a strengthened professional organisation. Working with him as managers are Jim Richardson and Elizabeth Sayers, dealing with charitable fund and Government grants respectively. Elizabeth has continued to bear responsibilities in this capacity, under considerable pressure, for many years. Penny Hassell, who was previously responsible for charitable fund grants, gave valuable service in this capacity.

An occupational therapist has been appointed to assist with the assessment of the needs of applicants for grants.

Applications procedures

People applying for grants are asked to complete an application form, giving information about their disability, their physical measurements, the car and adaptations required, and their household and financial circumstances. Cases are submitted and recommendations prepared by the office, accompanied by the application form and other supporting documents. A great deal of painstaking work by the staff is required in preparing these submissions, involving detailed costings of vehicles and adaptations, and often lengthy discussions with applicants, who can sometimes be difficult and demanding. The same work is needed in dealing with the charitable fund cases, which are in general settled by the staff, although the research is usually in less depth because the solutions are less complex.

In some cases a report by a mobility centre, such as the Banstead Mobility Centre, is needed to assist Motability in establishing the precise requirements of the applicant. Motability also employs Steve Hodgson, working from the Mobility Advice and Information Service (MAVIS) of the Department of the Environment, Transport and the Regions, as an assessor, carrying out a complete assessment of all applicants for Drivers Fund grants both at MAVIS and on a peripatetic basis. Sometimes the applicant has been to a mobility centre and is able to submit its report; in other cases the assessment is called for by Motability, the cost being borne by the appropriate fund.

Motability relies heavily on these reports in considering the more difficult grant applications, and it has built up a close working relationship with the centres. Regular meetings are held with the Forum of Mobility Centres to discuss the information needed by Motability, the form of reports and other matters of mutual concern. Motability and the Forum have established a system of accreditation for the mobility centres. In this work Morigue Cornwell of the Banstead Mobility Centre, Ann Mells of the Mobility Advice and Vehicle Information Service and Mike Quinn played an essential part. A list of the accredited centres is given in Appendix 5.

In the early years of grant giving, Motability sometimes arranged a home visit by a social worker to confirm the need for a particular vehicle or to go into family circumstances. A group of social workers from the Family Fund was recruited for this purpose. They built up a valuable expertise in dealing with applicants, and although their services have been replaced by two of Motability's own visitors, their help was greatly appreciated.

EXAMPLES OF GRANTS

Examples of grants from the three funds, with case histories are given in Appendix 6. The grants from the charitable fund described were made some time ago, and they do not necessarily reflect the changes outlined in this chapter.

TECHNICAL PROJECTS

Mike Richards also has on his staff, as Technical Projects Controller, Jim Kerr, who joined Motability in 1994, bringing extensive experience in the provision of vehicles for disabled people in New Zealand.

Technical Projects have involved the establishment of standards for adaptations to vehicles for which grants are made. This ensures that mobility centre reports provide the information required by Motability, and that significantly adapted vehicles are inspected by an independent team of contracted inspectors before delivery, to confirm that they meet the customer's and Motability's requirements.

In addition, follow-up customer surveys are carried out one month and ten months after delivery. These ensure that any problems are identified at an early stage so that they can be rectified during the warranty period.

This work has involved the setting up of a Vehicle Adaptation Project Procedure, the emphasis being on quality service to the customer. Work has also begun on a code of practice and a programme of accreditation for vehicle conversion specialists.

These procedures are an integral part of Motability's continuous quality improvement programme, which is aimed ultimately at providing the right vehicle first time and every time, and supplying customers with vehicles which are fit for the purpose of use, with particular attention to safety, functionality, reliability and the dignity of the user.

10

THE MOBILITY EQUIPMENT FUND AND DRIVERS FUND SURVEY 1995

In 1992 the Technical Committee commissioned surveys of people who had received grants for cars from the Mobility Equipment Fund, in order to gauge whether the most suitable vehicle was funded i.e. whether the Fund was being put to the best possible use. Two surveys were carried out by the Transport Research Laboratory (TRL), with the assistance of the Mobility Advice and Vehicle Information Service. The first survey was covered in a report in 1993 by Marian Edwards, and the second in 1995 by Tracy Savill and Richard Stait. The second report, which is dealt with in this chapter, deals with the Drivers Fund as well. The questionnaires used in this second survey were almost identical to those in the previous survey, with a question added to ascertain the level of satisfaction with the service provided by Motability.

Motability is indebted to the TRL for the valuable information provided by these surveys.

An earlier survey of adaptations in 1989, also commissioned by the Technical Committee, is described in Chapter 13.

SUMMARY OF THE 1995 REPORT

The final section of the 1995 report provides a convenient summary of the findings of the survey. This is reproduced here, and is followed by a fuller account, extracted from the whole report: 52 drivers and 113 passengers returned their completed questionnaires. 79 per cent of these people found the adaptations fitted to their vehicles to be satisfactory. Some of those who were not satisfied mentioned that the adaptations were not suitable for them, some because their physical condition had deteriorated. The passengers cited ramps as the main cause for discontent (7 people), and 5 passengers were dissatisfied with the wheelchair clamps. In addition, 11 passengers mentioned poor ride comfort as a problem, especially in terms of making the journey painful. These results are similar to those found in the 1993 survey, where ramps and wheelchair clamps were the main problems.

The drivers and passengers had used their vehicle for a range of activities over the previous six months. As well as being able to conduct their own affairs, such as going to the bank or shopping, people also used the vehicle for social reasons. These included visiting friends and relatives and having days out.

A large number of people said that having the vehicle meant they could now have the independence to go out when they wanted. This had meant new opportunities for them, such as acquiring a job or doing voluntary work, being able to go out as a family and providing lifts for other people, some of whom were also disabled. A major benefit for the passengers was the ability to get into a vehicle without transferring from their wheelchair. This was easier for both the passengers and their carers, some of whom were no longer physically able to lift the passengers. These findings are encouraging in that they show how the vehicle has not only enhanced people's own lives but also those of the people around them. For many, it meant a release from the confines of their home.

Helping disabled people to travel more frequently and further afield has economic benefits: they said they were able to go out shopping and have holidays and days out, and in addition, they were less reliant on the health and social service transport and home visits by doctors.

80 per cent of the people said that they were satisfied with the service provided by Motability. However, 17 per cent of the sample said that the paperwork took a long time to be

processed, and some people experienced problems with getting information or answers to correspondence.

GENERAL INFORMATION ABOUT RESPONDENTS

Of the 72 questionnaires sent to disabled drivers, 52 were returned, giving a response rate of 72 per cent. 37 were male and 15 female. Six were aged 25 or under, and 47 were 65 or under. 47 said that they were the main driver of the vehicle.

Of the 164 questionnaires sent to passengers, 113 were returned – a response rate of 69 per cent. 63 were male, and 50 female. 56 were aged 18 or under, and 108 were 65 or under. In 64 per cent of the cases, one or both parents were named as the main driver of the vehicle. A quarter of the vehicles were mainly driven by the disabled person's husband or wife.

DRIVERS

Amount of grants

The average amount the respondents said the MEF or the Drivers Fund had contributed to the cost of the vehicle was £6,392. The maximum total cost of the vehicle was £30,000, with an average of £13,995. Nearly half of the drivers had used their savings to supplement grants from the Funds and their mobility allowance, and additional help had been obtained from other charitable organisations in 29 per cent of the cases.

Adaptations

All the 52 vehicles had been adapted in some way, many with more than one adaptation. The numbers of vehicles with the most common adaptations were as follows:

	Number
Hand controls	28
Manufacturer's power steering	26
Tailor-made power steering	22

83

Steering ball	23
Powered/servo brakes	20
Modified parking brake	19
Electric wheelchair tie-down	16
Adapted seat	15

Joysticks were fitted in four vehicles.

The respondents were asked to say whether they found the adaptations satisfactory, and to give a brief explanation if they were not content. 71 per cent of the drivers said they were satisfied, and 5 people failed to give an answer. The reasons given for dissatisfaction were as follows:

	Number
Adaptations do not meet my needs/make driving difficult/give me muscular aches	5
Poor quality or fitting of adaptations	3
Transferring back to my wheelchair is difficult	2
Condition has deteriorated so that adaptation(s) no longer meet my needs	2
Poor value for money	1
Insufficient power generated	1
Vehicle is left-hand-drive when I wanted right-hand-drive	1

Quality of life

Among the 52 drivers, the main uses of the car more than once a week were:

	Number
Visiting friends or relatives	29
Shopping, bank, post office, etc.	26
Evenings out	11
Paid employment	10

12 people said they had a job before obtaining the vehicle, and 7 of these felt the vehicle had helped them to retain their job.

In addition, 4 people said the vehicle had helped them to get a job.

32 drivers said that the way in which the vehicle was most useful was in giving them freedom and independence and saving them from being housebound. 19 listed going out when and where they wanted as something they could not do before having the vehicle, 9 visiting people and 8 going out alone.

Among the comments made about the use of vehicles were these:

I can be my own man and not have to rely on anyone.
I do not feel trapped inside my home – I feel free.
I can get in and out of the vehicle without any assistance and go shopping on my own.
Hospital appointments can be kept without using hospital transport.
I can visit the countryside with family and friends and take my father to visit relatives far away and off the public transport route.
Before I had my Metro I had an Invacar (a trike), so I was unable to take my relations and friends out.

A very gratifying finding was that over two-thirds of the drivers said that being mobile had enabled them to help other people, including taking out friends and relatives, giving lifts to other disabled people and doing voluntary or charity work.

PASSENGERS

Vehicles chosen

A third of the passengers had been provided with a Renault or Nissan Versa, 15 per cent with a Renault Trafic and 15 per cent with a Fiat Fiorino. 88 per cent had vans and 7 per cent 'high tops'. (As some 'high tops' are derived from vans, it is possible that some people said that their vehicle was a van when it should have been classified as a 'high top'.)

Amount of grants

The average amount said to have been contributed from the MEF was £4,176. The maximum total cost of the vehicle was £18,000, with an average of £10,927. In 22 per cent of the cases a contribution had been made from savings, and additional help had been obtained from another charitable organisation in 16 per cent of the cases.

Adaptations

97 per cent of the vehicles had been adapted, the most commonly used firms being Widnes Car Centre (34 per cent), Universal Mobility (24 per cent) and Gowrings (10 per cent). The numbers of vehicles with the most common adaptations were:

	Number
Wheelchair ramp without winch	53
Wheelchair ramp with winch	32
Tail lift	24
Mechanical wheelchair tie-down system	24
Modified seat belt	16
Extra seats	11

These figures are taken from the information supplied by the respondents, and it may not match what they had actually been given.

82 per cent of the passengers were satisfied with the adaptations. The main reasons for dissatisfaction were as follows:

	Number
Problems with ramps	7
Problems with wheelchair clamps	5
Problems with winches	4
Poor view/lack of visibility	2
Poor ride comfort	2
Lack of internal space	2

Among difficulties experienced by passengers were:

	Number
Poor ride comfort	11
Ramp and electric winch needed Ramp too steep or too narrow	8
Wheelchair unstable	6

Quality of Life

The purposes for which the vehicles had been used more than once a week were as follows:

	Number
Shopping, bank, post office, etc.	58
Visiting friends or relatives	57
Days out	23
Attending school or college	23
Evenings out	14
Attending day or evening classes	12
Attending clubs	11
Medical visits	10
Paid employment	5

Only two people had a job before having the vehicle, but both said that it had helped them to keep their job. One other person said that the vehicle had helped them to get a job.

32 passengers said that the way in which the new vehicle was most useful was in enabling them to get in and out of the vehicle without difficulty and/or without being lifted. 43 said simply that they could now go out when and where they wanted.

Among the comments made by users or carers about the use of vehicles were these:

His life is now something other than sitting in a wheel-chair.
My own health has improved. (I was suffering from

severe shoulder trouble due to constant lifting of my daughter.) Days out for her are no longer something I dread.
When I go out it is when I want to, and distance is no longer a problem.
I can now see other things. Before I could only see the dashboard and the top of windows.
My wife was trapped indoors because she could not travel in a conventional car and we live in a rural area without public transport.
Without a vehicle our son would be housebound, as public transport is totally out of the question.

90 per cent of the people said that if they had not been able to go out in their vehicle they would have needed to rely on other people or services more, such as Health and Social Services transport and home visits, special transport services, such as Dial-a-Ride, and friends and relatives. This is an interesting confirmation of the 'cross benefits' of the Motability Scheme in relieving pressure on publicly-provided services.

40 per cent of the passengers said that being mobile helped them to help other people, for example by providing lifts for other disabled people, and for people more generally.

DEGREE OF SATISFACTION WITH THE SERVICE

77 per cent of the drivers and 81 per cent of the passengers thought the service provided by Motability was satisfactory. The most common critical comments were these:

The paperwork took a long time to be processed – 13 drivers and 15 passengers
The vehicle was not entirely suitable – 6 drivers and 4 passengers

These figures should of course be seen in conjunction with

those given above about dissatisfaction with vehicles and adaptations.

Some of the more critical comments are reproduced below:

It was a struggle to obtain proper information and a lot of red tape to reach the right person.
A Government-run fund could have been more supportive.
It was a very long-winded procedure, and my mother already has a lot to do with me being so disabled.
A little slow in answering correspondence and phone calls.

It should be pointed out here that much of the delay in making grants arose from the necessity to maintain a waiting list because of the limited amount of money available. Time is also needed to establish exactly what adaptations are required, and to make sure that the large grants being asked for from public money are genuinely needed. This does not of course remove the obligation on Motability to keep people fully informed about the progress of their applications and the reasons for delays.

Some people made very positive comments, such as:

We cannot say 'thank you' enough to Motability for all their help.
Very high praise for all administration at Harlow.
Excellent, efficient service.
If it hadn't been for Motability I could never have managed.
Most helpful from the start.

FOLLOW-UP ACTION BY MOTABILITY

Motability took action to meet the main concerns raised by the survey, relating to the suitability of the vehicles and adaptations provided and the time taken to deal with applications. As to the first question, many improvements have since been made in this field as a result of the new procedures, described in Chapter 9, for assessment, the setting of standards and the inspection of vehicles. The same chapter sets out the steps taken to improve the processing of applications.

11

FUNDRAISING BY MOTABILITY

The Department's administration grant to Motability does not make any provision for the cost of fundraising, which has to come out of the money raised. This is in accordance with the agreed division of responsibility between the Department, MFL and Motability in 1977, which gave the charity the task of creating a charitable fund to pay for grants to disabled people whose allowance was insufficient on its own to provide for the car they needed.

For the first eight years of Motability's operation this charitable fund was sufficient to meet all requests for grants. But even though the net funds raised annually grew from £68,508 in 1978–79 to £433,976 in 1993–94, it eventually became necessary for three other funds to be created in order to support Motability's own efforts. These were the Tenth Anniversary Trust Fund, the Mobility Equipment Fund and the Drivers Fund, all of which are dealt with in Chapter 8. There has at the same time been steady progress in direct fundraising by Motability, which in 1996–97 met over 40 per cent of the expenditure on charitable grants.

1978–1985

Motability began its fundraising operation in 1978 by appointing as Head of Fund Development Tom Petzal, who had worked for Lord Goodman and Lord Sterling in raising money for the Queen's Silver Jubilee Fund. Frank Coven also gave his services as a consultant. A small fundraising office, which was also responsible until 1992 for Motability's general publicity, was set up in London. Through the generosity of the P & O Group, premises and services for this office were provided free of cost, first at 4 Carlton Gardens, Pall Mall, and later at 77 New Oxford Street. This facility, and the support of the P & O staff, were of great help in keeping down fundraising expenses and so increasing the proportion of the income raised directly available for grants.

Appeals to companies and trusts

The first major event in the fundraising programme was a banquet held in 1979 in aid of Motability at the Mansion House in London, presided over by the late Sir Kenneth Cork, Lord Mayor of London. Sir Kenneth, who was a Member of Motability, had named Motability as his charity of the year. This event, attended by opinion leaders in the City of London, provided a springboard for the system of direct appeals to companies which has always been a key part of Motability's fundraising activities.

Motability is indebted to all those companies, trusts and individual donors who have so generously contributed to the funds and helped in other ways since 1978. It would be impracticable to name them all, but a list of supporters is given in Appendix 4. Many gifts have been made by covenant or under the Gift Aid Scheme, giving additional benefits by way of repayments of tax.

Special events

Other special events in the early years included a film premiere attended by Princess Alexandra; a concert at St James's Palace in the presence of HM the Queen; in collaboration with the Douglas Bader Foundation; a concert at the Albert Hall (Sir Douglas Bader was a Member of Motability until his death in 1980); a television appeal by the racing motorcyclist, Barry Sheene.

Collection boxes

To reach the general public, it was decided in 1981 to start a collection-box scheme. After consultations with a company specialising in this form of fundraising, it was commissioned to place and empty boxes in shops and public houses, first in a pilot area, which produced promising results, and then countrywide. After initial success the scheme proved a disappointment, and despite attempts to improve it over the years, it was finally necessary for Motability to take it over directly and to wind it up in 1988. However, the boxes are still in use on special occasions, such as the Horse of the Year Show and Motorfair, at which substantial sums have been raised, and at other fundraising events.

Motability North-West and Motability Kent

In 1984 Motability began to explore the possibility of raising funds regionally. A voluntary organisation, Motability North-West, was set up in Manchester for this purpose. Led by a local businessman, Jonathan Taylor OBE, Motability North-West collected considerable sums of money, especially through projects in schools and carol concerts. Wendy Robinson in the Fundraising Office was closely involved in this work, and the organisation in the schools was undertaken by Sylvia Giness, who rendered valuable service over many years in this and other ways, with particular success in making Motability well known in the North-west.

With the retirement of Jonathan Taylor, Motability North-West was led by the President, Sir Sidney Hamburger, and the Chairman, Brian Lingwood.

In 1997 it was reluctantly decided to wind up the organisation because, in spite of all the efforts of the Committee, the amount of funds raised had been found not to justify the administrative costs involved. At the same time, Motability expressed its gratitude to the many people who had worked so hard on its behalf.

In 1984 and 1985 similar arrangements were in operation in

Kent, thanks to generous help from William Brake of Brake Bros and his committee, which raised a large sum for the charity.

Boxing

In 1986 a small group of friends of Motability decided to organize a boxing evening, the proceeds of which would go to the charity. From modest beginnings this has become an annual event which has produced some of the largest single donations to the charitable fund, averaging over £30,000 a year. Tim Gooch, a Member of Motability, conceived the original idea and ably managed the event until 1991, since when he has been assisted by the Boxing committee under the chairmanship of John Beverton.

Motability Enterprises Limited

In 1984 Motability set up a company, Motability Enterprises Limited (MEL) to handle the finances of fundraising events. The income generated is paid to Motability under deed of covenant. In the year ended 31 March 1997 this amounted to £803,333. The directors of MEL are Allan Beard, Noel Muddiman and Richard Cowell.

1985–88

In 1985 it was decided that more formal arrangements than hitherto were needed for the oversight of fundraising and publicity. A Charity and Public Relations Committee was therefore set up under the chairmanship of Allan Beard and later of Alan Outten.

Roly Stafford, formerly Head of Public and Press Affairs of BP Oil, played an important part in the work of this Committee, particularly in connection with public relations and the design of appeal literature and promotional material.

Motability owes a great debt of gratitude to him, not only for this work, but also for his services as a Governor and member of the Grants Committee and the Executive Committee from 1977 until his retirement from active work in 1991. He received an OBE for his services to disabled people through Motability and a number of other charities.

For some years the task of the Committee and the Charity Office was two-fold: to raise funds, and to establish the name of Motability in the minds of the general public and potential benefactors so as to create an understanding of its work. In 1992 separate arrangements were made for publicity and public relations, as explained in Chapter 12, and the committee became the Fundraising Committee. After the establishment of an enlarged fundraising organisation, reporting directly to the Executive Committee and later to the Board of Governors this committee was no longer required. In effect, its functions have been largely taken over by MEL.

In 1985 Tom Petzal left Motability to take up an appointment with another charity. Nigel Haygarth took his place on a voluntary basis, working part-time, shortly after his retirement from a senior management post with BP. The appointment provided an opportunity to review the work of the office, and to make full use of the new Director's business experience it was decided to concentrate on direct appeals rather than special events. Nigel Haygarth rationalised the programme of appeal letters, and as a result the income from donations rose from £167,905 in 1985–86 to £349,580 in 1988–89.

Motability Midlands

Under Nigel Haygarth's guidance a fundraising committee was set up in Birmingham in 1987 – Motability Midlands – with Baroness Fisher as President and Stan Jefferson as Chairman. Accommodation and services for the committee were provided free of charge by Bristol Street Motors. After providing valuable support to Motability, the committee was disbanded in 1995.

95

Broadcast appeals

In 1988 Sir Richard Attenborough, a Governor of Motability, broadcast a very successful radio appeal for the charity. Two years later he presented a television appeal which was equally successful. The script for these and Barry Sheene's appeal in 1984 were the work of Roly Stafford,

Christmas cards

In the same year Joyce Acher, wife of the Vice Chairman of the Executive Committee, took on the sale of Motability's business Christmas cards, at which she worked tirelessly and with great success. Her efforts not only produced substantial sums for the charity but added to the public awareness of Motability's work. The sale of Christmas cards is now managed by the Fundraising Office and continues to contribute to Motability's funds. Over 70,000 cards were sold in 1997.

1988–1993

After a successful period in the Charity Office, Nigel Haygarth decided in 1988 to move on and enjoy his retirement. He had worked with great dedication, and it was with sadness that Motability learned of his death in 1992. The work was passed on until 1989 to Berick Dale, also retired from BP, who gave his support on a voluntary basis.

Tom Petzal and his successors had enjoyed the support of Hilary Finch, who was closely involved in all the fundraising activities and the administration of the Charity Office from 1984 until 1989. Hilary had computerised the system of appeal letters, bringing the work into the office – previously it had been handled by an agency – before the arrival of Nigel Haygarth. The database of information about companies and grant-giving trusts has been kept continuously up to date, providing the basis of personalised appeals letters.

When Hilary left to broaden her experience in another

charity, she was replaced by Alison Fleming, and later, from 1991 to 1992, by Phillip Bush.

Help from the Department

Motability received a special non-recurring grant of £50,000 from the Department in 1986 in order to cope with a shortfall in the charitable fund. Later there was a Government grant of £190,000 as a result of an incorrect calculation of the Retail Prices Index, which had led to underpayments of Social Security benefits, including the mobility allowance, which could not be traced to individuals.

The lead-free petrol campaign

During 1989 a campaign, organised through MEL was mounted to promote the use of lead-free petrol. It was launched at Buckingham Palace by HM the Queen, with all-party support, and made a major contribution to lifting the sales of lead-free petrol from around 5 per cent to over 25 per cent of total sales by the end of the campaign in October 1989.

The campaign raised the general profile of Motability and made the media, motoring organisations and the general public more aware of its work for disabled people. The campaign's funds had all been provided by voluntary contributions from business and industry specifically to promote the use of lead-free petrol, and there was no cost to Motability's funds. There was a balance of £44,312 at the end of the campaign, which passed from MEL to Motability's charitable fund.

Motability Scheme cars, numbering at the time over 47,000, which were capable of adaptation were converted to run on lead-free petrol, usually at no cost to the user. Because of the lower price of this fuel, the change was of financial benefit to users as well as improving the environment.

Other contributions

Payments were received from Equity Insurance Limited under an arrangement for a return of a proportion of the profits made in the operation of its off-road insurance scheme for Motability users.

Fleet News, a paper catering for the car fleet trade, organised a fundraising operation, involving the donation of ex-fleet cars for auction in aid of Motability, which raised over £60,000.

Mike Quinn, at that time Grants Section Manager in the Harlow office, began a series of Golfing Days in aid of Motability, which continues to raise substantial sums.

HANDING-OVER CEREMONIES

The public handing over of Motability Scheme cars, with the agreement of the recipients, to which the press, radio and television are invited, has proved to be a valuable means of making Motability more widely known, and in particular of assisting fundraising operations. On four occasions Motability has been honoured to have these presentations carried out by HM the Queen as Chief Patron of the charity:

1981 at Buckingham Palace, when the event was filmed for the Queen's Christmas broadcast.
1988 at St James's Palace, to mark Motability's tenth anniversary.
1991 at Buckingham Palace, to mark the delivery of the 250,000th Motability Scheme car.
1995 at the Mobility Roadshow at Crowthorne, to mark the delivery of the 500,000th Motability Scheme car.

The ceremony in 1991 was held in the courtyard of Buckingham Palace, where the Queen met 14 disabled people and their families and handed over the keys of their cars. They were afterwards entertained to tea inside the Palace together with the other guests. These included the Secretary of State for Social Security and the Minister of State for Social Security and Disabled People; Patrons, Governors, and other members and staff of Motability; representatives of the Department, the

Clearing Banks, MFL, motor manufacturers and dealers, Motability's Technical and Regional Committees; and other supporters and helpers of the charity.

The handing over in 1995 was preceded by the launch of the NFC Lifestyle/Young Disabled Drivers Scholarship by the Secretary of State for Transport. This scheme gives grants to learner drivers through Motability.

The 500,000th car supplied under the Motability Scheme was handed over by the Queen in 1995 to a disabled former soldier, Richard Hickmott, in the presence of a number of distinguished guests, as at the 1991 ceremony. Afterwards she was introduced to Motability staff and to supporters and disabled users of the Motability Scheme who had participated in the '500 Roads to Freedom' fundraising campaign. Certificates were presented to these participants by the Chairman of Motability, Lord Sterling, and they were guests that evening at a celebration dinner.

On other occasions Motability has also been greatly helped by public handing over ceremonies carried out by Ministers, Members of Parliament and other well-known people, which have helped to publicise Motability's activities and its need of funds.

Plans are now being made for the handing over of the millionth Motability Scheme car at the end of 1998.

1993 ONWARDS

The consultants' review

It became clear in 1992 that, even with the help of the Tenth Anniversary Trust Fund, a large increase in Motability's charitable income would be needed to keep pace with the ever-increasing calls for grants. With the generous support of Shell UK, the Fundraising Committee under Alan Outten therefore commissioned a study by a firm of charity consultants of the possibility of enlarging the income.

The consultants' report recommended fundamental changes in the fundraising organisation which were examined by a special group set up by the Executive Committee. As a result, steps were taken to create an enlarged and more professional organisation.

Premises

The new organisation proved to be too large to be accommodated in the P & O premises, and it moved in 1993 to an office in Southwark Bridge Road in London, which was provided free of charge by MFL. A further move took place in 1995 to an office, again rent-free thanks to the National Westminster Bank, in Margaret Street, London. In 1996 the office moved to Motability's headquarters at Harlow.

Senior management 1993–1995

In 1993 Joanna Lewis was appointed to the newly-created post of Director of Fundraising on secondment from KPMG. She had already done a great deal of work in this field for Motability, and her skills in fundraising had been demonstrated at the International Show Jumping Championships at Olympia in December 1992. By the use of the commitment of the volunteers whom she had recruited, and an imaginative approach to corporate sponsorship, some £93,000 was raised over the five days of the championships – substantially more than any other charity had raised before at the event.

Joanna had also been largely responsible for the introduction of a completely new and up-to-date logo for Motability, with the theme of 'On the road to freedom' which was introduced into all Motability's letter paper and publicity material. It was launched at the London Motorshow in the presence of the Minister for Disabled People and many stars of TV and radio.

Lifestyle *magazine*

One of the most notable achievements of the new organisation was the launching in 1993 of Motability's award-winning quarterly *Lifestyle* magazine, which is mailed directly to the homes of all Motability Scheme customers, free of charge. The costs of the magazine, which is a full-colour 52-page publication with a circulation of over 360,000, are met partly by advertising revenue. It is produced by Killen International Partnership, which has entered enthusiastically into its production.

While providing regular information on the Motability Schemes, and reviews of the cars available, the magazine seeks to reflect the diverse interests and aspirations of disabled people in the context of the family group and the community. At the same time it aims to provide additional benefits to customers and their families – e.g. by negotiating as a group. It fosters the concept that the disabled people who receive it are not just customers, but members of Motability.

By inviting readers to write to the magazine, Motability has established a direct dialogue with its customers about all aspects of the schemes, customer service and fundraising opportunities. The response has been very encouraging. Several projects have been launched through the magazine, including the Friends of Motability Club and the NFC/Motability Young Disabled Drivers Scholarship, enabling young disabled people to learn to drive, which is funded by the NFC Foundation.

Natalie Pearse, formerly Motability's Head of Public Relations, was mainly responsible for the launch of *Lifestyle*.

In 1994 Joanna Lewis returned to KPMG. Motability is indebted to her for the way in which she built up an organisation which transformed the fundraising operation to meet the growing demands on the charity. As a result of her leadership, the net income from fundraising rose by over 60 per cent between 1992–93 and 1993–94, from £265,155 to £433,976.

NEW DEVELOPMENTS

The move of the fundraising office to Harlow made it possible to integrate the fundraising work more closely with that of the rest of the organisation, under the overall control of Motability's Director. At the same time, it was necessary to recruit and train a new team.

In October 1995 Hazel Gotfraind was appointed to head the fundraising organisation. She joined the charity from Killen International, where she had participated in the production of *Lifestyle*. She has had great success in introducing new ways of fundraising, and as a result the net income in the year ended March 1997 rose to over £700,000.

Under her management the key factor underpinning the growth of the office has been the securing of corporate sponsorship to cover operating costs. There have also been substantial improvements in the targeting of company and trust appeals, and the introduction of selected merchandising and trading initiatives, such as the Motability Household Insurance Scheme.

The main elements of the strategy developed by the new Director of Fundraising are these:

Direct appeals to the public
There are now over 20,000 people, including standing order donors and covenantors, who have made donations and become 'Friends of Motability'. Largely through the help of members, over £15,000 was raised in a national Motability raffle.

A legacy campaign was launched in 1997, when Motability's Will Guide 'Safeguarding the Future', which is sponsored by Royal & Sun Alliance, was published. In the first six months over 5,000 requests were received for the guide.

By special arrangement with Shell, donations to Motability can be made by people using the Shell Smart Card when buying petrol. The company has also supported Motability in other ways.

Appeals to companies and trusts
These continue to be an important source of income, but it is sometimes difficult to convince potential benefactors that the existence of the Tenth Anniversary Trust Fund,

which is primarily needed to provide for potential future commitments, does not remove the need for funds to assist current applicants.

Special events
There has been a continuous build-up of the events programme to enhance the profile of Motability. This has included the launch of Motability's 'On the Road to Freedom' video, 10,000 copies of which were distributed free of charge to disabled people and their carers. This was sponsored by Vauxhall.

There was also the Bardolino Wine Run, with Motability user Kate Hill being first through the Channel Tunnel in the *Daily Mail* Le Walk.

Other events have included, or will include, musical evenings at the Law Society, golf days sponsored by the RAC and Canons Brook Golf Club, and the Motability Rated Stakes at York Races sponsored by the AA.

Trading
This includes insurance services, the sale of Christmas cards to companies and private buyers, flowers by post in conjunction with Flying Flowers, and other special offers in *Lifestyle* magazine.

Through the efforts of Mrs Gloria Jackson, who has a Motability Scheme car, a special rose named 'The Road to Freedom' was produced in aid of the charity and launched at the 1996 Hampton Court Flower Show, selling over 500 plants in its first season.

Contributions from companies doing business with Motability
Until recently the AA was an important contributor in the form of a return of payments made for roadside assistance cover in leases for cars already covered by arrange-

ments made by the manufacturers with the RAC.

Substantial help has been given by Nissan, Renault UK and Eagle Star.

Royal & Sun Alliance currently donate a percentage of the profits made in insuring cars.

Employee fundraising
Successful employee fundraising initiatives have been developed with the AA and Royal & Sun Alliance.

The Peking to Paris Run

In September 1997 Gerry Acher, Vice Chairman of Motability, drove his vintage 1932 Aston-Martin car in the Peking to Paris Run, marking the 90th anniversary of the first and greatest motor race of all time. He and his co-driver were one of the 66 teams out of the original 90 competing which completed the hazardous journey. They covered 17,000 kilometres in 45 days, and they were presented with the Spirit of the Rally Cup for capturing the essence of the 1907 race.

In making the run, Gerry raised over £150,000 in sponsorship in support of Motability's charitable fund and the Macmillan Cancer Relief Fund.

12

CONSTITUTIONAL AND ORGANISATIONAL DEVELOPMENT

Motability was incorporated in January 1978 as a private company limited by guarantee and registered as Charity No. 299745 under the Charities Act 1960. In May 1988 it was granted a Royal Charter. This provides, like the original Memorandum and Articles of Association, for Governors, other members and officers, and sets out as Motability's main objective 'to facilitate the relief and assistance of disabled persons in connection with the provision to the beneficiaries of personal or other transportation'.

Her Majesty the Queen is the Chief Patron of Motability, and there are a number of other distinguished Patrons. Lord Goodman and Lord Sterling were the founding Chairman and Vice-Chairman respectively. In 1994 Lord Goodman became President and held this office until his death in 1995. In 1994 Lord Sterling became Chairman and Gerry Acher Vice-Chairman.

Motability is controlled by its members, who appoint Governors from among their number at their Annual General Meeting. The Governors constitute a Board which manages the charity's affairs.

Present Patrons, Governors and Members are listed at the beginning of this history book. Motability is grateful to the many distinguished people who have served in these capacities in the past.

THE GOVERNANCE OF MOTABILITY

From 1978 to 1996 the Board of Governors delegated responsibility for the running of Motability to certain of its members constituting an Executive Committee and appointed annually. (This committee was originally known as the Joint Working Party.) In 1996 the Board decided to take more direct control of the work, meeting quarterly instead of annually and subsuming the responsibilities of the Executive Committee.

Responsibilities of the Executive Committee

The Committee exercised a close control over the business of Motability. It received detailed reports and statistics each month from the sub-committees, the Director and the Chief Executive of MFL, and approved the administration budget, the annual accounts and the annual report. It selected and appointed the senior staff, determined the salary structure and supervised the fundraising and grants operations. Above all, it monitored the operation of the Motability Schemes and made changes in them as necessary, such as new insurance contracts and agreements with the motoring organisations.

Membership of the Executive Committee

It was recognised when Motability was first set up that it would be essential for people with an intimate knowledge of the mobility needs of disabled persons to be closely involved in its overall control. Three disabled Governors were therefore appointed and made members of the Executive Committee from the outset. They have served on it ever since. These are Sir Peter Large, Joe Hennessy and Adrian Stokes.

Peter Large was invited to serve because he was Chairman of the Joint Committee on Mobility for Disabled People (the JCMD), and also because he had led a successful campaign to secure the inclusion of disabled passengers as well as drivers in the mobility allowance scheme. The Committee comprises the representatives of some 28 national organisations of and for people with mobility handicaps. Peter Large was made a CBE in 1986 and knighted in 1993 in recognition of his many services to disabled people.

Joe Hennessy and Professor Adrian Stokes were and are active in many organisations of disabled people, including the Disabled Drivers Association and the Disabled Drivers Motor Club respectively. They have both been awarded the OBE for services to disabled people. Joe Hennessy is now Chairman of the JCMD.

Further representation of the needs of disabled people was secured by the inclusion as a founding member of George Wilson CBE, who until 1990 was the Director of RADAR and, as explained in Chapter 1, was involved in the original concept of the leasing scheme. He retired from the Committee in 1991, but continued to serve as a Governor.

Roly Stafford, who had given great help to Motability from 1978 onwards, and became a Governor in 1990, served as a member of the Committee in 1990 and 1991.

Alan Outten, formerly Deputy Chairman of MFL, attended Committee meetings from 1990 and served as a Governor and full member from 1992 until his death in 1996. He had given great service to Motability, and has been much missed.

Allan Beard, as the responsible Under-Secretary in the Department, attended meetings of the Joint Working Party until his retirement from the Civil Service in 1979, when he became a Governor and Committee member. He served as Hon. Treasurer from 1985 until 1998 when his place was taken by Sir John Quinton. His services for disabled people were recognised by the award of the CBE in 1994. Until 1990 he chaired meetings of the Committee in the absence of Lord Sterling; thereafter Gerry Acher, who had become a Governor and Committee member, took over this duty.

Gerry Acher first became involved with Motability as a partner in KPMG, the auditors of the charity's accounts. In this capacity he was of great help in the building up of closer working relationships with MFL and a greater understanding of its finances, and also in the forecasting of future demands on the charitable fund.

After he became a member of the Executive Committee his work for Motability greatly increased, and his appointment as Vice-Chairman in 1994 recognised his crucial role in the charity at a time of expansion and increasing complexity in its operations. Without the immense amount of time and energy which he has devoted to the work, on an entirely voluntary basis, it would have been impossible for Motability to become the large and professional organisation which it is today. In view of his position in Motability, the auditing of the accounts was taken over from KPMG by Coopers and Lybrand.

All the people mentioned above have faithfully served Motability as Governors over the years, giving up a great deal of their time and energy without payment.

Supporters of the Executive Committee

There have always been other people in attendance at meetings of the Executive Committee who, although not participating in its decisions, have been able to take a full part in its discussions. Motability is grateful for their contribution to its work. In the early years these included Victor Adey (representing the Clearing Banks), Frank Coven and Tom Petzal (responsible for fund development), and David Morris and Peter Brinton of KPMG, who were especially helpful in advising both Motability and MFL in the development of the first leasing scheme.

Joanna Lewis of KPMG played an important part in the work of the Committee by carrying out strategic studies and in the development of the fundraising work.

There has been a continuous liaison between Motability and those responsible for policy in the Department, who have always given valuable help and support. Thanks are due to those who have assisted the Committee over the years by attendance at meetings, notably Peter Askins, Michael Caddick, Ron Croasdale, Ken Eckersley, Claire Edwards, John Harley, Graham Hart, Kevin Holton, Bob Layton, Barry Matthews, Jack Nairn, Ruth Siemaszko, Bill Taylor and Neil Ward. Claire Edwards was particularly helpful in handling the many complicated negotiations with the Department made necessary by recent developments.

Motability is grateful to these and all the other officers of the Department who have helped the charity since its inception. One important aspect of this work has been the close cooperation between Motability, MFL and the Benefits Agency on arrangements for verification of the award of allowances, their payment to MFL and the issue of the Motability leaflets to recipients of the allowance. The Agency was also very helpful in issuing questionnaires for the survey described in Chapter 7 and the illustrated guide issued in 1991 and 1992.

There is of course a close working relationship between Motability and MFL, which is explained in earlier chapters, but it should be mentioned here that over the years its successive representatives have also given valuable service by attending meetings of the Committee: Bill Armstrong, Mike Austin, Tony Gourlay, Harry Hall, Brian Hassell, John Jackson, Ed Lester and Malcolm Titchener.

Meetings of the Executive Committee

The Committee, which held its first meeting in February 1978, met monthly – once a fortnight until 1986. From 1978 until 1990 the meetings were held in a conference room provided by the P & O Group at 4 Carlton Gardens, Pall Mall, but they later took place in a room made available by KPMG at Salisbury Square. Motability is grateful to these two organisations for providing these facilities.

INTERNAL REVIEWS OF MOTABILITY'S WORK

In 1990 the Executive Committee decided that, after 12 years of operation and given the very rapid recent growth in Motability's activities, the time had come to carry out a review of the organisation. A report was commissioned from KPMG and presented by Joanna Lewis in August 1990. The report made a number of recommendations which were followed up by the Executive Committee.

It was decided that the growth in the range and complexity of the work made it essential that the Executive Committee should take on more of a strategic role, the detailed work being delegated to other committees and to project teams. These teams would include members of the management of Motability and MFL. There was a long-established Technical Committee (see Chapter 13), and the Grants Committee, dealt with in Chapter 9, had recently been set up to relieve the pressure on the Executive Committee. In addition, it was decided to set up a Marketing Committee (later renamed the Customer Affairs Committee, and described below) and to reconstitute the Charity and Public Relations Committee as a purely fundraising committee. Project teams have since studied a number of questions, including insurance.

The report recommended that each of Motability's committees should draw up a detailed plan for its work, setting the tasks in order of priority and specifying the call which each would make upon resources. These plans were assembled into an overall plan and system of priorities which was kept under review by the Executive Committee.

The review was followed by strategic studies of the organisation of the office. As a result, the staff dealing with grants was strengthened by the creation of the post of Overall Grants Manager, supervising the two officers responsible for grants from the charitable fund and the Mobility Equipment Fund respectively. The appointment of a Public Relations Officer also followed from this study.

A Coordinating Committee, composed of representatives of the clearing banks, MFL and Motability, was set up to examine methods of improving the integration of the work of Motability and MFL, including the creation of improved information systems and a common database.

The Customer Affairs Committee

The Customer Affairs Committee was set up in 1990. Its main function was to consider improvements in Motability's services and in the ways in which those services were made known to

110

potential customers. Much of its work involved the commis-
sioning of the 1993 customer survey described in Chapter 7,
and it was also concerned with public relations. Among those
who served on the Committee, under the chairmanship of
Allan Beard, were Adrian Stokes, Mike Austin of MFL, Mike
Bowkett of Perrys, Gwilym Bennett of Ford, Gus Killen of
Killen International Ltd, and members of the staff – Irene
Bass, Cathy Davies, Joanna Lewis, Kevin O'Loughlin and
Natalie Pearse.

The Committee ceased to function when its work was superseded by changes in the organisation from 1995 onwards.

THE SENIOR MANAGEMENT

The work of Motability's original Secretary, Barry James, was
described in Chapter 2. Having been seconded from the
Department, he reached retirement age in March 1982, but
continued in his post in a part-time capacity. On his final
retirement in October 1983 he was able to hand over a thriving
organisation to his successor, Ken Keen, also seconded from
the Department.

Ken Keen presided over a rapidly expanding operation, and
in 1988 he was given the title of Director in recognition of his
increased responsibilities. In particular, he had organised the
move to Harlow and planned and introduced from 1985
onwards a computerised method of dealing with applications,
without which it would have been impossible to cope with the
growing volume of work. As a result, Motability's administrative costs per vehicle supplied were steadily reduced – over the
ten years to 1993 they fell from £51.37 to £26.59. (In real
terms, the reduction was even greater.)

Until 1994 there was a post of second in command of
Motability. Gwen Allen held this position as the first Deputy
Secretary of Motability from 1978 to 1980. (Motability learned
with regret of her death some years afterwards.) She was
succeeded by Geoffrey Barrett until 1983, and he was in turn
replaced by Gerald Priestley until 1987. These three officials

had been seconded from, and returned to, the Department, but the next appointment to the post was made by promotion from among the staff of Motability, when Robin Taylor was made Assistant Director in 1987. He left in 1994, after seven years of devoted service.

Ken Keen retired in May 1993, having given outstanding service for nearly ten years, and shortly afterwards he was made an OBE in recognition of his services to Motability. During his period of office no less than 300,000 cars were supplied. His place was taken by Simon Willis, who was seconded from the Department.

Simon Willis built up a close rapport with the disabled people's organisations concerned with mobility, and there were many expressions of satisfaction with his work in this field. He worked closely with MFL in the planning of a new common computer system, leading to greater efficiency and a better service to customers. He also prepared a new business plan for the charity, providing for a better-staffed, better-paid and more professional organisation. The business plan involved a number of new managerial appointments, in addition to that of the Director of Fundraising

The Finance Director's post was the first to be filled, in June 1994, by Graham Moss, who came from Nissan (UK) Ltd. He was heavily engaged from the outset in improving the accounting methods and financial controls at Harlow, negotiating the budget with the Department and working closely with MFL in the planning of the new computer system.

Cathy Davies became the Operations Director in November 1994, with the task of controlling the whole system for dealing with applications for cars and wheelchairs, involving close working relations with MFL, car manufacturers and dealers, the insurance companies and motoring organisations. Cathy, who came from the Ford Motor Company, was able to contribute invaluable experience of the motor industry.

In 1995 Simon Willis's period of secondment from the Department ended, and Noel Muddiman CBE was appointed as Director in August of that year, having assisted Motability for some months beforehand. He came to the charity on his

112

retirement as a Brigadier in the Army, where he had held the post of Commandant of the Army School of Mechanical Transport. In this position he had extensive experience with motor vehicles, and as well as commanding soldiers, he employed a number of civilian personnel. He therefore brought a range of valuable experience to his new post, and was well fitted for the task of reorganising Motability to cope with its rapid expansion, and the recommendations of the National Audit Office (see Chapter 14). The development of the charity under his leadership is described in Chapter 15.

Public Relations

The reconstitution of the Charity and Public Relations Committee as a committee dealing solely with fundraising marked a decision to bring publicity and public relations generally under a newly-appointed Head of Public Relations, responsible to the Director of Motability.

This change was made because Motability, in both its fund and its car-supplying activities, had grown to such an extent that it could no longer manage without someone able to take overall responsibility for the charity's public relations. The duties of the post include taking active steps to publicise Motability, dealing with and advising on criticisms of the service, handling promotional material of all kinds (including stands at exhibitions) and advising on relations with customers.

Motability is indebted to the Government for agreeing to make the services of a Civil Service information officer, Natalie Pearse, available on secondment to undertake these duties. She took up her post in November 1992, and provided valuable help to Motability. The post of Press and Public Relations Manager is now held by Anne-Marie Chatterton.

Motability publishes an Annual Report giving a full account of its work during the previous financial year. It includes 14 pages of financial information, which the Finance Director, Richard Cowell, has brought fully into line with the new requirements imposed on all charities by the Charity Commission. Since 1995 there has also been included a five-page

113

detailed explanation of the way in which Motability's schemes work, written by Gerry Acher.

Whatever may have been said by critics in the past, Motability cannot now be accused of a lack of transparency in recording its activities.

OFFICE PREMISES

For the first few years the Motability central administration office was in London. It was first set up in premises made available by the Department in a Government building, State House, in High Holborn, and moved to another Government office, the Adelphi, near the Embankment, in December 1979. In December 1981 it moved to commercial premises at Boundary House, Charterhouse Street.

Motability had always found it difficult to compete with other employers in the recruitment of staff, and this was accentuated in 1986, when the rapidly rising volume of applications made staff increases necessary, creating difficult working conditions in the cramped premises. This led to a disturbing rise in the turnover of staff. Motability was also faced with a large increase in rent, which it would not have been possible to meet out of the Government grant for administrative expenses. It was therefore decided to look for other premises outside London, and in May 1987 premises were secured in the centre of Harlow. In 1989 the further rise in applications following the removal of car tax from Motability contract-hire cars made it necessary to rent additional office space close to the main office.

The move to Harlow involved the loss of many members of the staff who were not willing to move out of London, compensation for those who moved but had higher travelling expenses, and the recruitment of new staff. The success of the move soon became apparent in better working conditions, an overall improved quality of staff and much reduced turnover of staff. There was a noticeable improvement in morale, one example of which was the participation of the staff in the

114

Family with a disabled child meeting Motability's Chief Patron Her Majesty The Queen at the celebration of the 250,000th Motability Scheme vehicle at Buckingham Palace 1991. Also present, Sir Nicholas Scott (right).

The late Diana, Princess of Wales visiting the Motability stand October 1991 at the Motorfair, accompanied by Gerald Acher Esq, Vice Chairman.

In 1993, former Prime Minister The Rt Hon John Major hands over a new vehicle, specially adapted for Christine Stockton and family, at 10 Downing Street to celebrate the 350,000th Motability Scheme vehicle. Also seen here, Gerald Acher Esq, Vice Chairman (left) and Gwilym Bennett, Manager of Ford 'Motability' Administration (centre).

July 1995, Richard Hickmott was surprised to learn he was the Motability Scheme's 500,000th customer. Her Majesty the Queen presented the keys of his new vehicle at the Mobility Roadshow, Crowthorne, Berkshire.

December 1996, Alistair Burt MP, former Minister of State for Social Security and Disabled People, handed the keys to Shelley Rosenfield when she picked up her Motability Scheme vehicle. Shelley passed her driving test after completing the Young Disabled Driver's Scholarship. A unique partnership between Motability, The NFC Foundation and BSM (British School of Motoring).

Noel Muddiman CBE, Director, launches the 'Customer First' initiative at the Mobility Roadshow, Crowthorne, 1997.

The Prime Minister Tony Blair with his wife Cherie presenting a vehicle to Motability Scheme customer Mark Potter and wife Julie at the London Motorshow, Earls Court, 1997.

Example of one of Motability's most advanced vehicle adaptation projects, a high tech drive-from-wheelchair project incorporating four way electronic joy stick control for accelerating, breaking and steering which also includes voice control for operation of indicators and gear sclection. Completed in July 1997.

Harlow Festival, raising over £2,000 in 1991 for the charitable fund.

Later, however, increases in the volume of work, leading once more to unsatisfactory working conditions, made it necessary to look for new office premises, and the search for these was put in hand by Simon Willis. Further developments are explained in Chapter 15.

13

TECHNICAL DEVELOPMENTS

It was recognised from the inception of Motability that steps to bring the opportunity of motoring to as many disabled people as possible would call for two parallel processes. One, which has already been described, was to devise schemes which would put cars within the financial reach of allowance recipients. The other, equally important, was to carry out work which would stimulate changes making it possible for disabled passengers and drivers to travel in greater safety and comfort in their vehicles, and further, to enable those who could not previously make use of a car to contemplate doing so.

The work would include adaptations to existing vehicles so as to improve the means of access for both passengers and drivers, the controls used by drivers, and the means of loading and stowing wheelchairs. A particular concern was the adaptation and design of vehicles which disabled people, whether passengers or drivers, could enter without getting out of their wheelchairs.

THE TECHNICAL COMMITTEE

These functions were originally included in the remit of a Finance and Technical Committee, which later became the Vehicle Committee under the chairmanship of Sir Barrie Heath. In 1978, after a review of the role of this committee, it was superseded by a Technical Development Committee, chaired by Professor Adrian Stokes, which first met in March 1979.

In July 1988 the Committee was reconstituted as the Technical Committee, continuing under the chairmanship of Adrian Stokes. This Committee, reporting to the Executive Committee, normally met once a month. Its terms of reference were as follows:

To investigate items of equipment which aim to provide personal mobility, with special reference to those items which can be provided through Motability, and, as appropriate, to make recommendations for further action. To investigate technical issues arising from the provision of equipment for personal mobility, and, as appropriate, make recommendations for further action. To initiate development of equipment where it felt that there was a need for such equipment.

In June 1997 the Committee was again reconstituted as the Technical Advisory Group, with similar terms of reference. A list of people who gave valuable service as members of the Committee and its predecessor during the period from 1979, and of the members of the Technical Advisory Group, is given in Appendix 9.

THE WORK OF THE COMMITTEE

New equipment

The Technical Development Committee initiated the development of a number of items of equipment. The first was the Motahoist, which enabled a severely disabled person to transfer from a wheelchair into a sliding seat in the front of a car. The seat was then slid into the driving position and the wheelchair pulled into the vacant space. This conversion was produced commercially by David Hodge and Son Ltd.

The second development was a steering wheel knob which, in addition to assisting with steering, allowed the driver to use the minor controls without removing his or her hands from the

117

knob. While a number of prototypes were made, this device did not enter commercial production.

The third, and major, development was the application of modern electronic technology to vehicle control. In a three-phase programme funded by the Department, a car was converted to minimal-effort controls so that the accelerator, brake and steering could be used by means of a single control, with virtually no effort. This development was completed satisfactorily but so far, although considerable interest has been expressed, it has not been taken up commercially. The completed vehicle was demonstrated on the BBC television programme *Tomorrow's World*.

Vehicles and adaptations

The Committee was concerned with ensuring that drivers and passengers are assessed for the most appropriate vehicle and adaptations for their needs. An early paper by the Committee provided input to the Department of Transport, which led to the setting up of their Mobility and Vehicle Information Service (MAVIS). The Committee was involved in Motability's discussions with the Forum of Mobility Centres, in order to improve communications between the centres and Motability, particularly in connection with grants from the Mobility Equipment Fund. As explained in Chapter 9, a programme has been set up for the accreditation of the centres.

A survey was carried out in 1989 to assess the degree of satisfaction with the Motability Schemes, with particular reference to adaptations. 3,000 questionnaires were issued to people who had had a car for one year – i.e. those who would be likely to be able to answer questions about their early impressions of the vehicle. The response rate was 63 per cent.

Of the respondents, 37 per cent were drivers, 35 per cent were passengers, and 28 per cent said that they were sometimes drivers and sometimes passengers. 7 per cent of the cars had power-assisted steering, and 22 per cent automatic transmission.

It was found that 12 per cent of the cars had been adapted

for drivers, and 2 per cent for passengers. Of those with adaptations, 14 per cent of drivers and 17 per cent of passengers had had trouble with those adaptations.

The survey provided the basis for a continuing study of adaptations, together with the scope for improvements in assessment, advice to customers and design and fitting.

In 1993 and 1995 surveys commissioned by the Committee were made of people who had received grants for cars from the Mobility Equipment Fund and the Drivers Fund. The object was to find out whether the most suitable vehicle and adaptations were being funded – i.e. whether the grants were being put to the best possible use (see Chapter 10).

Van conversions

Neil Wood of Birmingham University, a member of the Committee, produced a report on vans for use by disabled people, dealing in particular with adaptations. The report discusses among other things modifications to controls, such as hand controls and joystick steering; means of access to the vehicle, including lowering of the suspension, side lifts and tail lifts; and the lowering of floors to accommodate the driver's or passenger's wheelchair. It has proved to be of considerable value in discussing improvements with manufacturers.

One of the difficulties of driving a van from a wheelchair is that the driver's seated height may prevent him or her from having a clear view through the windscreen. In some cases this may be overcome by the lowering of the floor of the van or by the use of a special wheelchair, but both of these devices are expensive. Fortunately, it proved possible to fit a raised windscreen to Ford Transits, which overcame the problem in some cases, but this was not an ideal solution, and other possibilities have since been examined.

Rear-access vehicles for drivers

There are several comparatively inexpensive adapted vehicles on the market with a ramp at the rear for access by disabled passengers in their wheelchairs. Unfortunately, there is as yet no such vehicle for drivers who are confined to wheelchairs: if they wish to drive, they normally need the vans described above or a large car with a side or tail lift and other adaptations. Where the customer cannot meet the cost of such a vehicle himself, there is a call on the Mobility Equipment or Drivers Funds and a heavy drain on their resources.

The Technical Committee therefore considered whether a less expensive vehicle, possibly with access from the rear, could be produced for such cases. It examined a number of vehicles which might serve this purpose. These included the Elswick Envoy and the Invashrew (both now out of production), the Nuova Amica and the Gateau.

The Gateau, manufactured in France, is a four-wheeled vehicle with access doors at either side and a rear door. It is designed to be driven from a wheelchair, entrance being from the rear via an electro-mechanically operated door and a floor which lowers to ground level. The floor is then raised and the wheelchair locked into posi-tion for driving. There is provision for a limited amount of luggage and for a single passenger in a fold-down sideways-facing seat.

Motability is grateful to Robert Glossop, a Committee member, for arranging for this vehicle to be imported and demonstrated in this country. Disabled people who tried it were enthusiastic about the basic concept, although a number of mechanical and other improvements appeared to be needed. The Medical Devices Directorate of the Department of Health carried out an appraisal on behalf of the Committee, which has been discussed with the French manufacturers. Unfortunately they were not interested in supplying the Gateau in the UK, and since the evaluation they have ceased production. Discussions have taken place with British manufacturers, who expressed an interest, but who understandably required a reliable estimate of the demand for the vehicle.

The Cranfield University study

The Committee therefore commissioned through Motability a study of the user requirements and market potential for a purpose-built vehicle of this kind. It was carried out by a group headed by Philip Oxley from the Centre for Logistics and Transportation of Cranfield University, with the aid of a grant made by the Tenth Anniversary Trust Fund. What follows is taken from the report of this study, which was presented in July 1996.

The research was divided into two principal elements. First, a large-scale postal questionnaire survey was mounted, in which 1,530 wheelchair users provided information on a range of matters related to their personal mobility, use of cars as drivers or passengers, and their views on the importance of a car capable of being driven from a wheelchair.

The most important conclusions drawn from the first, large-scale survey were as follows:

The importance of being able to drive from a wheelchair
A quarter of the respondents considered this to be very important; a further 9 per cent thought it important.
Proportionately more women than men (31 per cent compared with 21 per cent) considered it to be very important.
People with long-standing, progressive disabilities were more likely to consider it to be important than were those with disabilities resulting from accident, injury, or other 'one-off' events.
Young people, up to the age of 30, contained the highest proportion (46 per cent) who thought it important or very important.

Design characteristics of the vehicle
Just over 56 per cent considered it important or very important that the vehicle should be of normal appearance.
Again, the greatest stress on the importance of normal appearance was found among the youngest drivers.
Most people would like the vehicle to have three or four passenger seats.

121

Vehicle cost
The range of prices people said they would be willing to pay for a vehicle capable of being driven from a wheelchair was very wide (from £1,000 to £65,000). The mean price quoted was just under £10,800, with median and modal values of £10,000.
Taking the figures given by those people who considered the ability to drive from their wheelchairs as very important produced a higher mean price (£11,782)

The views expressed by this large sample of wheelchair users suggested that there was a potential market for a wheelchair-driveable car, a potential further emphasised by the problems which the respondents experienced when using cars, by far the commonest of which related to difficulties in getting in and out of cars and loading and unloading wheelchairs.

The second survey concentrated on 100 people, all of whom expressed interest in a vehicle that could be driven from a wheelchair. 68 of these respondents were drivers (31 driving from their wheelchair); the remaining 32 travelled as passengers, but had expressed an interest in driving.

The conclusions reached in this second part of the study were:

The majority of respondents would prefer a small/medium hatchback of standard appearance.

Access to the vehicle would be from the rear, preferably by ramp rather than by lift, provided that the space requirement and ramp angle could be minimised.

The base vehicle should be available with standard hand controls and with other, secondary controls in easily-operated standard format. For a minority (around 10 to 15 per cent) high gain/low effort primary controls and infra-red secondary controls would be required.

The vehicle should have automatic transmission (manual as an option) and power-assisted steering.

To provide users with good access to servicing and maintenance facilities, the vehicle should be derived from a volume-produced vehicle from a manufacturer with a substantial network of dealerships.

Vehicle cost is a critical issue: the target cost to the purchaser should be of the order of £12,000, a figure which is regarded as reasonable by 30 per cent of the survey respondents.

The report concluded that in considering the commercial development of a vehicle to meet the requirements shown by the study, it would be prudent to assume that only half of those who appear from its theoretical calculation to be in the market for the vehicle would in fact buy it. This would mean a market of 300–350 vehicles a year. It then made proposals for a further study, including the selection of a volume-produced small/ medium car and the conduct of an engineering/design feasibility study on this vehicle, to determine more precisely how it could be modified for access and driving from a wheelchair.

It was suggested that the vehicle could not only meet a requirement in Great Britain but also meet a demand elsewhere in Europe, and that if there was a will to do so, Britain could take the lead in Europe in this field.

This is a very valuable report, whose recommendations have led to further study of the subject with the aid of an additional grant from the Tenth Anniversary Trust Fund.

Electric wheelchairs

A Code of Practice was developed for suppliers of electric wheelchairs, the acceptance of which was made a condition of doing business with MFL. The Committee monitored complaints about chairs acquired through Motability. The Code of Practice has been incorporated in the First Class Suppliers Charter (see Appendix 8).

The Committee was long concerned about reports of disabled people who had acquired wheelchairs through Motability which turn out to be unsuitable. On the initiative of Morigue Cornwell, a member of the Committee, a practical guide to choosing a wheelchair was produced and issued by Motability.

123

Code of Practice for dealers

The Committee developed a Code of Practice for dealers supplying, servicing and maintaining Motability Scheme cars, which was formally launched at the Motor Show in October 1993. It included such matters as access to premises, parking, courtesy and replacement cars, and staff training in the needs of disabled people. Acceptance of the Code was made a condition of recognition as a Motability dealer. The code has been superseded by the First Class Suppliers Charter.

Other matters

The Committee considered a wide range of other subjects, including:

In-car telephones.
A Fair Wear and Tear Guide to assist in deciding whether damage to a car returned at the end of a contract hire agreement should be regarded as acceptable to the dealer.
Demonstrations of new products.
The safety of hand controls on manual cars.
Procedures for controlling and approving the fitting of adaptations.

THE EQUAL MOBILITY PROJECT

Through inspections carried out by Jim Kerr as Technical Projects Controller, Motability became aware of the volume and varying quality of adaptation work being carried out on manufacturers' vehicles. Most of these manufacturers did not appreciate the scale or nature of the adaptations.

Motability therefore proposed a collaborative partnership involving Motability, the Department of Transport, motor vehicle manufacturers, mobility centres and vehicle conversion and adaptation specialists, to provide a national focus for all aspects of improved personal mobility for disabled people including the initial design of vehicles. This Equal Mobility

Project would also benefit the very large number of elderly drivers and passengers.

Discussions about the project have begun with motor manufacturers, and the Tenth Anniversary Trust Fund has made a grant of £100,000 to help to set it up. The aim of the project is to bring about coordination and improvements in research and development, assessments, adaptations, and training programmes for assessors, adaptation specialists and Motability staff.

14

MOTABILITY UNDER ATTACK

Throughout 1995 and 1996 a sustained attack was made on Motability in newspapers, *Disability Now*, radio (the BBC programme *Does He Take Sugar*), television (Channel Four's *Dispatches* programme) and Parliament.

The main thrust of the attack took the form of allegations that the banks were making excessive profits out of the Motability Schemes, with the implication that Motability's Governors, who had overall responsibility for those schemes, had failed in their duty to disabled people.

Among the Parliamentarians who took part in the campaign against Motability was Alan Simpson MP. He made a particularly virulent attack in the House of Commons, saying that, 'We must not allow a sleazy bunch of bankers and benefactors to make themselves a fast buck through a no-risk monopolistic scam, perpetrated on the backs of the public and the disabled' (*House of Commons Official Report* 19 July 1995, column 1618).

Without reference to the Executive Committee a report concerning Motability's operations (the Bircham Report) was prepared by a firm of solicitors and discussed at a meeting with the Charity Commission. The Charity Commission decided to take no action as a result of this meeting.

The report, which was highly critical of Motability, was subsequently withdrawn by the solicitors, who accepted that they had not been given the full story about the charity. However, the allegations were so serious that the Governors decided to commission an in-depth examination of the report by a sub-committee of Governors, chaired by Sir Peter Large, but not including Lord Sterling and Gerry Acher, who had been the particular subject of criticism. The sub-committee reported that in their opinion Motability was operating in an entirely proper manner, and that allegations which had been made of illegality were entirely unfounded.

The public attacks on Motability had an unfortunate effect on fundraising, and thus on the funds which were available for grants. Understandably, companies and trusts were reluctant to make donations to a charity which had been accused of allowing commercial organisations to make money out of disabled people.

EXAMINATION BY THE NATIONAL AUDIT OFFICE

Quite independently of these allegations against Motability, the National Audit Office (NAO) had decided in 1995 to undertake an examination of the charity. It was entitled to do so because ultimately the money used by allowance recipients to obtain cars comes from public funds, and also because of the annual grant which the Department makes to Motability to cover the costs of its administration.

It was not surprising that, after nearly 20 years of Motability's activities, the NAO should include this examination in their programme. Predictably, it was suggested by the critics referred to above that the investigation had been asked for by the Department because it shared their concerns about the charity. However, Lord Inglewood, speaking for the Government, made it clear in the House of Lords on 15 June 1995 that this was untrue.

The task of the NAO was to examine whether the Motability Schemes provide value for money to disabled people, and the steps Motability had taken to improve value for money and the management of the schemes.

Motability greatly welcomed the examination, which it was confident would provide firm and independent evidence that all the allegations made against it were unfounded. In the event, this was exactly what happened.

127

THE NAO REPORT

The report of the NAO was laid before Parliament on 18 July 1996 (HC 552 Session 1995–96). The Press Notice issued by the NAO, which is reproduced below, provides an authoritative summary of the Report.

Sir John Bourn, head of the National Audit Office, today reported to Parliament that the 'Motability Scheme offers good value for money to disabled people'.

The Motability contract hire scheme offers vehicles at a price significantly lower, by an average of 30 per cent, than those charged by other contract hire companies to large fleet operators.

The contract hire and hire purchase schemes are particularly useful to those on low incomes who might not otherwise secure a lease agreement or loan.

Competition has been used to obtain services which account for 70 per cent of the cost of the Scheme. Motability are now reviewing if, and how, competition for the remaining 30 per cent – the financing and administration services provided by Motability Finance Limited – might be introduced, and whether this would be beneficial to customers.

The Report concludes that Motability, the charity responsible for the Scheme, can build on the action they have taken, since 1994, to improve customer service through:

greater transparency in setting out the standards of service disabled people can expect to receive;
systematically measuring the quality of service actually provided;
better monitoring of the performance of the Scheme and of the operations of Motability Finance Limited.

Sir John is pleased to note that Motability are implementing measures to address these issues.

The NAO also investigated various allegations about conflicts of interest involving the Vice-Chairman of Motability. The NAO could find no evidence of any conflict adversely affecting the charity. Other main findings in the report are:

each year Motability review the level of the profit margin earned by the banks which finance the Scheme. The profit margin has varied over the lifetime of the Scheme. In recent years Motability have negotiated reductions in the banks' profit, from 2 per cent in September 1993 to 1 per cent on new agreements from January 1996. In the year to September 1995 the banks earned £15,600,000 before tax, £10,500,000 after tax, on their total funding of £1,200,000,000 to the Motability Scheme;

since 1988 the prices charged under the Motability Scheme have included a contingency margin to build up a contingency reserve, to provide against the risks involved in running the Scheme. This is normal business practice. The contingency margin has been reduced progressively from 1 per cent in 1994 to 0.5 per cent from June 1995, and has been removed from April 1996 as a result of more stable economic conditions;

since the late 1980s reserves have built up which have exceeded the amount considered necessary to safeguard the Motability Scheme. As the return made by the banks who fund the Scheme is restricted to a management fee and an agreed profit margin, surplus reserves totalling £35,000,000 have been transferred over time to the Motability Tenth Anniversary Trust Fund. The Trust invests these funds to provide Motability with money to make grants to disabled people and for research. In September 1995, it was decided that £26,900,000 of the contingency reserve was surplus to the Scheme's immediate requirements. However, the decision to remove the contingency margin on new contract hire agreements from April 1996 will result in this surplus being used to reduce prices for all customers entering an agreement from that date by approximately £80 over the three years of a typical con-

129

tract hire agreement. This will include the 66 per cent of existing customers who typically renew their agreements;

disabled people may apply for a grant from Motability towards the cost of obtaining or adapting a vehicle. Motability have generally been able to provide a decision within six months for those seeking charitable assistance, but where vehicles require major adaptation for severely disabled people from the Mobility Equipment Fund, the waiting time for a decision increased from 12 to 18 months. In February 1996 Motability revised the criteria for making grants to relieve some of the pressure on the Fund;

Motability have taken steps since 1994 to improve services by investing in new computer systems and setting out codes of practice for some aspects of their work. However, Motability do not yet measure systematically the quality of service provided to disabled people by either themselves or Motability Finance Limited;

Motability have increased the information they provide to customers on the operation of the Scheme. But more could be done to provide feedback on the performance of Motability and Motability Finance Limited.

The NAO Annual Report for 1997 contained the following reference to Motability:

The Motability Scheme involves organisations in the public, voluntary and private sectors working in partnership to assist disabled people to obtain personal transport. Our examination resulted in the first, detailed independent account of the way the Scheme operates, and our recommendations built on work that Motability had in hand to enhance good value and service for the future. As a result of action by Motability to strengthen their oversight of the Scheme and work by their principal service provider, Motability Finance Limited, to take advantage of changes in economic conditions, customers entering into new contract hire agreements in 1996 will

130

benefit from price reductions worth around £26,900,000 over the period of their agreements.

REVIEW BY THE CHARITY COMMISSION

The complaints against Motability led the Charity Commission to carry out a review of its operation independently of the NAO.

The result of this review was announced in a News Release on 18 July 1996, in which the Commission announced that it was satisfied that there was no evidence to support any of the various criticisms which had been levelled at the charity. The Chief Charity Commissioner, Richard Fries, said that they were satisfied that Motability used its resources properly to provide a unique service for disabled people. The review concluded that:

the terms upon which vehicles are supplied to disabled people through the Motability Scheme are better than those available to individuals from other suppliers. Good progress has been made in the use of benchmarking and market testing to ensure that the charity's beneficiaries receive value for money. The Commission remains of the view that the trustees should benchmark or market test at regular intervals;
there is no evidence to indicate that either the banks or MFL have made excessive profits from the operation of the scheme;
the Vice-Chairman of Motability, Mr Gerry Acher, has not derived any personal benefit from payment for work carried out for the charity by the accountants KPMG, in which Mr Acher is a senior partner;
KPMG's services have been supplied on terms which are advantageous to Motability;
changes to the format of Motability's accounts and reports have made the workings of the scheme much more transparent to beneficiaries and to the general public; and

131

the charity's management structure has recently been reviewed to improve customer service and to meet the demands of continued growth.

The Commission said that in the course of the review the conduct of the charity and its trustees was examined closely. Charity Commission staff visited Motability's offices and interviewed trustees and employees.

THE RESPONSE TO THE NAO AND CHARITY COMMISSION REVIEWS

In a Press Release issued on 18 July 1996, Motability said that the NAO Report had made several important and very helpful recommendations for improving the service and administrative performance of Motability, most of which had been, or were already being, implemented. These could only improve Motability's service to its customers.

The reports by the NAO and the Charity Commission were welcomed by Motability as giving it the opportunity to proceed with its development and its customers the assurance that they were not, as had been suggested, being exploited. In particular, the Governors of Motability were pleased that the unfounded allegations made against the integrity of their Vice-Chairman had been proved to be without foundation.

Most of the newspapers which had published criticisms of Motability reported the favourable outcome of the reports, although not, it must be said, with the same amount of prominence. So far, the radio and TV programmes which had attacked Motability have not issued any corrections.

Some critics seemed determined to continue their attacks, although in a lower key, notably by suggesting that improvements in the Motability Schemes were made only because of criticisms, and that the report confirmed the 'huge financial improvements' supposed to have been made during the draft stages of the report. In fact, as the NAO Report acknowledges, the reduction in the margin earned by the banks in their

132

lending to MFL, and in the contingency margin on leases, had been part of an ongoing process. This was made possible by the regular studies carried out for Motability by KPMG. In particular, the process of tendering for a new insurance contract, the results of which made possible improved contract hire terms for customers, had been set in train well before the NAO review was announced. Again, the NAO Report refers to more stable economic conditions as enabling MFL to remove the contingency margin. There is nothing in the Report to support the allegation that the NAO study obliged Motability to improve its terms for customers. This is made clear in the Annual Report of the NAO for 1997 quoted above.

What can be said is that the criticisms made Motability aware of the need for greater transparency in its operations; this led, for example, to the detailed explanation of the way Motability works in the Annual Report for 1994–95.

Motability noted with pleasure that some of the grant-giving and other bodies which had withheld their support from the charity during the NAO examination signified their intention to resume after the publication of the Report.

EXAMINATION BY MOTABILITY OF THE RECOMMENDATIONS IN THE NAO REPORT

The detailed recommendations in the NAO Report are set out below, together with the results of their examination by the Governors of Motability.

Review the scope for increasing the level of competition for the financing and administration services provided by MFL.
Following the initial reports by Schroders mentioned in Chapter 4, it was decided that the most beneficial method would be to introduce competition into each discrete element of the contract hire agreement. The initial vehicle price is already subject to market competition, in which manufacturers have continued to discount a broad range

of models. The Governors have, however, given approval to studies of the possibility of introducing competition into the maintenance of leased vehicles and the assumption of the residual risk on their value at the end of the lease period. Detailed investigations by MFL have shown that such measures would produce substantial savings, enabling Motability to provide disabled people with even better value for money.

It was decided that there was little merit in dividing up the work of MFL, which is a non-profit-making organisation, between competing companies, but selective benchmarking of MFL's administrative costs is being carried out by consultants.

As regards the final aspect of the possibility of competition – in the funding of the Scheme – detailed studies by Schroders have been presented to the Governors, and further work on this is being undertaken by a committee.

Undertake regular reviews of finance costs of MFL to monitor the appropriateness of the banks' profit margin.
These reviews, which have been carried out for several years, are presented annually to the Governors, and this process will continue.

Set out in a formal agreement with the banks the use of any reserves generated by the scheme.
An agreement was signed in December 1997.

Set customer service targets for the services Motability and MFL provide, and monitor performance against them.
A full description of the steps taken to implement this recommendation is given in the next chapter.

Specify the performance measures that Motability will use to assess the services provided by MFL.
This has been implemented.

134

Set out clearly in a revised agreement with MFL the roles and responsibilities of the organisations involved in the Motability Scheme, and secondly the information the Governors require to fulfil their responsibilities.

The revised agreement was signed in 1996 (see Chapter 4).

Provide key performance information to disabled people using the Motability Scheme.

The Customer First initiative described in Chapter 16 has been fully reported in *Lifestyle*, and regular performance information will be given in the quarterly issues of this magazine.

EXAMINATION BY THE COMMITTEE OF PUBLIC ACCOUNTS

On 29 January 1997 the Committee of Public Accounts (PAC) of the House of Commons took evidence on the NAO report on Motability from the Permanent Secretary of the Department of Social Security, Dame Ann Bowtell DCB, and from the Director of Motability. The Minutes of Evidence, together with a great deal of supplementary evidence asked for by the Committee and provided by the Director, and further evidence by the Comptroller and Auditor General and the Permanent Secretary, were subsequently published as a Parliamentary paper (HC 444, Session 1996–97). The report of the PAC on its examination of the NAO Report and all the evidence given to it was published on 15 February 1998 (HC 444, Session 1997–98).

A formal response to the Report has been made by the Department and Motability.

The Report recognised the value for money of the services provided by Motability, and in general provided a fair and balanced account. It was surprising that a Press Notice issued by the Committee on its publication consisted almost entirely of criticisms of the charity and made no mention of the generally favourable findings in the Report.

There were however certain criticisms in the PAC Report, the most important of which are set out below, together with the response made by the Department in its formal reply.

Use of reserves

'... We are concerned that the Motability Scheme has generated substantial surplus reserves of £61.9m from the charges levied upon users, over and above the reserves of £19.3m deemed necessary by the banks to safeguard the Scheme. ... We urge Motability to ensure that if surpluses are generated in the future, they are identified and distributed as quickly as possible to those customers who contributed to them. We are surprised at these shortcomings, when Motability has been in operation for such a long time.

The Department notes the Committee's concerns. The figure of £86.7 million is the total of all reserves accumulated on the Scheme since its inception in 1977, of which £35 million was transferred to the Tenth Anniversary Trust and £26.9 million returned to customers through reduced lease charges. It is not practical to calculate surpluses on an individual lease basis, but around 65 per cent of leases are renewed, thus passing on the benefit to the majority of people who contributed to the surpluses. Reserves transferred from the Tenth Anniversary Trust help to meet advance payments for renewal as well as new cases, so there is also some measure of return there.

Reserves arose during the period that the economy was coming out of the recession from leases written during the recession. With stable economic conditions it is possible to more accurately cost lease prices. The Tenth Anniversary Trust has enabled Motability to remain secure during periods of unfavourable economic conditions. It is now adequate for the foreseeable future.'

Management of the Scheme

'We note the steps taken by Motability to strengthen their management; to establish quality service targets and to publish performance information which covers all providers to the Scheme; and to focus more directly on the needs of the customer and to seek customers' views regularly. We were surprised that such action had not been taken earlier in this Scheme's many years of existence. We look to Motability to build on the steps they have already taken to seek wider opportunities to get direct feedback from their customers.'

Motability was unable to devote as much of its resources as it would have wished to regular customer satisfaction monitoring in its early years because the necessary funds were not available. The entire scheme is now however driven by the Customer First Initiative.

Decisions on MEF grants

'We are concerned that it takes so long to take decisions on grants from the Mobility Equipment Fund, and that waiting times have deteriorated from 12 to 18 months. We look to Motability to bring the waiting time back to 12 months quickly, and then to seek ways of reducing it further.'

At the request of Motability's Governors the Trustees of the Tenth Anniversary Trust Fund made available £1,000,000 for the financial year 1997–98 which has made it possible to reduce the waiting time to 14 months. It is hoped that improvements in processes and staffing will bring this time down to 12 months in the next financial year.

The administration of the Drivers Fund involves the use of the limited capacity available among the small number of vehicle conversion specialists capable of carrying out the very complex work required. Some of these firms are unwilling to extend their capacity to the extent

137

required to improve delivery times until the result is known of the Government's review of the operation of the MEF and the Drivers Fund.

15

THE DEVELOPMENT OF MOTABILITY
SINCE 1995

The Board of Governors

In 1996 the Board of Governors assumed all the responsibilities which had been carried since 1978 by the Executive Committee. The strengthening and professionalisation of the senior management described below made it possible for the Board normally to meet less frequently than the Committee i.e. every three months. Between meetings full and detailed reports by the Director are sent to Governors every month, supplemented by separate papers as occasion arises. The Director is present at all meetings, and for part of the time other senior management staff, the Chief Executive of MFL and representatives of the Department are also in attendance.

An Audit Committee, composed of Governors, has been set up to maintain a review of a wide range of activities, including internal and external audits.

The new management

Since his appointment in August 1995 the Director, Noel Muddiman, has carried out an extensive reorganisation of the administration of the charity, in order to deal with the continuing growth in its business in a way which pays full regard to the needs of the disabled customers and of its staff. He has also introduced a number of important improvements in the services provided by Motability, including the formalisation of the regulatory oversight of those services. These changes, which are described below, can truly be said to have created a new Motability.

The Finance Director, Graham Moss, left in April 1995 to take up another appointment. He was ably replaced as a temporary measure by Robert Hibbert, seconded from KPMG. In September 1995 Richard Cowell was appointed to fill the post, and has proved a valuable asset. He is responsible for financial and support services.

A new post of Grants and Technical Director, filled by Mike Richards MBE, has been created to take overall charge of all aspects of grant giving, including the MEF and Drivers Funds, and the associated technical work.

Motability now also has a Fundraising and Marketing Director, Hazel Gotfraind. She is responsible for all aspects of fundraising, including special events, appeals to companies and trusts, and generally raising the profile of Motability in this field.

The Director has thus assembled a team of four Senior Executives, including Cathy Davies, the Operations Director, whose appointment has already been noted in Chapter 12, to support him in his work and to enable the charity to go forward with confidence into the next century. In addition he has set up a Support Executive which includes the Press and Public Relations Manager, Anne-Marie Chatterton, a Personnel and Training Manager, Barbara Hannant, a Project Executive, John van Dongen, and an Internal Auditor, originally Clifford Newton, now Tony Rozier.

The current management structure is shown in Appendix 11.

THE CUSTOMER FIRST PROGRAMME

In response to criticisms of Motability's customer service, the Director has introduced a comprehensive improvement programme under the title of Customer First. Its aim is to provide the highest standards of service for all Motability customers through a friendly and efficient service which is responsive to the views of disabled people. To meet this aim, a quality assurance programme has been implemented to deliver Motability's service against industry benchmarked standards for all existing and future customers. The programme has four main parts:

A Customer Charter, which has replaced the previous Code of Conduct in the handling of all customer enquiries.

A First Class Suppliers Charter, under which all dealers and retailers supplying cars under the contract hire scheme have to be inspected and accredited as 'First Class Suppliers'. This assures customers that when they see the official Motability Accredited sign, the company displaying it has met the standards set by the charity on their behalf.

A Customer Grievance Procedure, providing a properly structured avenue under which customers who are dissatisfied with any aspect of the Motability service can have their grievance properly addressed and answered.

A Customer Satisfaction Survey, to check regularly whether the customer service standards are those required by disabled people and meet their needs. The results are reported to all customers on a regular basis and will form a continuing part of the Motability programme.

The Customer First initiative was officially launched at the Mobility Road Show in July 1997. Encouraging reports have already been received from other organisations about the reduction in customer service complaints since the initiative began.

The Customer Charter

Under the Customer Charter, additional telephone lines and customer staff have been provided at both Motability and MFL to meet the new standards, and there is a training programme to ensure that the staff handle enquiries in a courteous and efficient manner. The aim is as far as possible for the two organisations to provide customers with a seamless service.

The linked information technology and telephone systems between Motability and MFL enable calls to be transferred from one organisation to the other without the need for the caller to redial.

In December 1997 all the Motability and MFL staff were given a Delineation of Customer Service Responsibilities document, clearly identifying the respective customer service responsibilities of the two organisations prior to the appointment of a Customer Services Director in MFL.

The heavy volume of business is shown in the following table of the average monthly levels of calls and written correspondence handled during 1997:

	Motability	MFL
Correspondence	6,000	4,000
Telephone calls	38,000	32,000

The Customer Charter standards for speed of response (see Appendix 7) were consistently met during the last six months of 1997.

The First Class Suppliers Charter

Under the First Class Suppliers Charter, minimum standards have been set and agreed with the motor manufacturers for facilities, premises and personnel. Dealerships in the Accredited dealer network are regularly inspected by Motability to ensure that the agreed standards are being consistently met. In addition, every Accredited dealership sends at least one member of its staff on a Motability Accredited training course. These courses enable Motability to ensure a consistent, current and thorough knowledge of all aspects of the Motability Scheme.

From April 1998, only Motability Accredited dealerships are allowed to supply cars on the contract hire scheme. Those dealerships which have failed to meet the required standards, or declined to join the programme, will not be used once their current hire contracts with customers come to an end.

The Charter has recently been extended to suppliers of

powered wheelchairs/scooters and to firms supplying vehicles and adaptations in grants cases. The full requirements of the Charter are set out in Appendix 8.

The Customer Grievance Procedure

The procedure is explained in a leaflet given to all customers, entitled 'Help Us to Help You'. It describes in detail how to make a complaint to Motability, MFL, or any of the service providers, and includes a code of conduct for the handling of complaints. These, including complaints of fraud and abuse, are dealt with by an Investigation Unit.

THE STAFF OF MOTABILITY

Motability's staff went through a difficult time until recently, working in largely unsatisfactory conditions to cope with an ever-increasing load of work. A warm tribute should be paid to them for the way in which they have performed in spite of all these difficulties and provided what has become a very satisfactory and prompt service to disabled customers.

In particular, a number of the longer-serving staff have shown their dedication to Motability by remaining with it during difficult times, and are now proud of being part of a professional organisation.

A particularly heavy responsibility has been carried by the staff dealing with applications for Motability Scheme vehicles, which have been running at the rate of about 150,000 a year, including answering all the many enquiries from customers and the relations with dealers. This work is under the supervision of Sharon Cunningham and Tony Rogers.

Under the new Director, a first job evaluation exercise and comparative pay study was undertaken in September 1995. There followed a three-stage programme to bring staff salaries up to the market rate, which culminated in the April 1998 pay award. In October 1997 the job evaluation and grading system was further refined, based on the nationwide Hay Evaluation

143

System. This has also provided the comparative data needed to assess the whole range of staff salaries against the national database incorporating the public, private and voluntary sectors and geographical area of employment. An intensive staff training programme has also been set up.

The present approved complement of staff is 212. This will inevitably increase because of the growth in business, but the increase will be kept down by improvements in efficiency.

PREMISES

An important task for the new Director was the completion of the search for new office premises. This resulted in the occupation from March 1996 of greatly improved quarters in a modern building close to Harlow station, which the lessors agreed should be renamed Goodman House as a tribute to the late President of Motability. These new premises, which have provided a greatly improved working environment, are expected to provide room for the continued growth in Motability's work well into the next century.

REVIEWS BY THE DEPARTMENT OF SOCIAL SECURITY

The Department has a responsibility for the public money flowing into Motability. This is not only a question of the grant provided for Motability's administration. In a wider sense, the Department needs to be satisfied that the very large sum made up of individual assignments of the Government allowance for cars is spent to the best advantage of the disabled people concerned.

Over the years the Department has carried out a number of reviews, staff inspections and audits of Motability and MFL. The last audit was in 1997, but an important review was carried out in 1994. Among other matters, the report of this review recommended that the informal understandings governing the relationship, accountability and financial controls between the Department and Motability should be formalised in a Financial Memorandum. It was also recommended that the agreement between Motability and MFL, setting out their respective roles and responsibilities, should be reviewed. These recommendations, which were also made in the NAO Report, have now been implemented.

FUNDING OF THE ADMINISTRATION

For 18 years the Department met the administration costs of Motability, not including the expenses of fundraising, in full, subject to annual budgetary negotiations. This was in recognition of the fact that without the Motability Schemes, the Government's aim to bring personal transport within the reach of all severely disabled people would not be possible. It meant not only that individual users' allowances could be devoted in full to the acquisition of their vehicles, but also that the funds raised by the charity could be used exclusively for charitable grants i.e. to assist people whose allowance alone was insufficient to pay for the car they needed.

However, the Department was faced in 1996 with the increasing cost of Motability's administration, arising not only from the growth in its business but also because of the cost of professionalising the entire system. Given the policy of cutting back on public expenditure, it became necessary for the Department to limit the grant for 1996–97 and the following year to the previous year's figure of £4,600,000.

It would have been unthinkable to reduce the scale of activity, for example by declining to entertain applications from some potential customers, in order to meet the deficiency in the grant. Accordingly, the Governors decided with reluctance that the shortfall in the grant would have to be met by incorporating a small element of the costs of administration into the charge for car leases. In 1996–97 this provided some £250,000 in additional funding.

145

16

TOWARDS THE MILLENNIUM

Growth in the number of allowance recipients

The measure of the success of the mobility allowance in bringing about personal mobility for disabled people is shown by the number of agreements for cars current in December 1997 – 340,639, which compares with about 50,000 trikes, cars and private car allowance recipients at the end of the old vehicle scheme in 1976. The difference is only partly accounted for by the fact that disabled passengers are eligible for the Government allowance, whereas they were excluded from the vehicle scheme. It is undoubtedly due mainly to the very large increase in recipients of the allowance – from 100,747 at the end of 1978 to 1,538,800 (including war pensioners) at the end of 1997. The growth over the years is shown in Appendix 2. This growth has so far shown no signs of abating – recipients of the allowance increased by 23 per cent during 1997. It is these people who make up the field of Motability's actual and potential customers.

As was explained earlier, the growth in the number of people receiving the allowance was undoubtedly affected by the assimilation of the mobility allowance into the Disability Living Allowance (DLA) in April 1992.

Growth in the number of users of Motability

As was to be expected, the increase in the number of allowance recipients described above brought about a rise in the number of users. However, this was far more than proportional: the number of car users rose from 14,744 at the end of 1982 to 345,525 at the end of 1997. This represented an increase from 5.9 to 22.4 per cent in the proportion of allowance recipients using Motability over the same period. This remarkable increase was undoubtedly due to the increasingly effective publicity given to the Motability Schemes and the continuing improvement in the terms offered over the years.

The Schemes are 'demand-led', i.e. Motability has no control over the number of applications it receives and must deal with. Moreover, because of the increase in the rate at which cars have been supplied on initial applications, there has been an ever-growing number of people with expiring hire agreements who apply again for another car. (Over 50 per cent of current applications are for the renewal of an agreement.)

However, there has been a falling-off in the rate of growth in recent months. Thus in 1997 the increase in applications over 1996 was 9.7 per cent, compared with the 17.5 per cent increase in the previous year. This brought about a slight reduction in the proportion of allowance recipients with Motability Scheme cars – from 24.2 per cent in 1996 to 22.4 in 1997. (There was a similar reduction in 1995, but this trend was reversed and growth continued in the following year.) This may well be no more than a temporary reduction in the rate of growth, but it is not at present possible to discern the reasons for the trend or to forecast whether it will continue.

The Department is at present carrying out a Benefit Integrity exercise in order to check the entitlement of a sample of benefit recipients, including those with the DLA. It is not yet apparent whether this will have any effect on the number with the benefit and thus the number of Motability Scheme users.

Growth in the supply of cars

In 1997, 137,509 cars were supplied, compared with 125,526 in the previous year and 9,712 in 1983.

The delivery in 1995 of the 500,000th car supplied by Motability since 1978 was a very important milestone in the charity's history. In spite of the trend in applications already discussed, it is expected that the 1,000,000th car will be delivered by the end of 1998, which means that in the space of three years the number of cars supplied will have doubled. The total fleet of cars currently on hire or hire purchase is now the largest non-public fleet in the UK, and double the size of its nearest competitor.

The proportion of total car sales in the UK represented by Motability Scheme cars varies from time to time, because although there is a steadily increasing number of purchases by MFL, the total of cars sold in the UK is itself a variable factor. The proportion is currently about 6 per cent over all manufacturers, and as much as 10 per cent for the most popular maker.

THE STRATEGIC PLAN

Motability has drawn up a strategic plan for its development over the next five years. The strategic aim is to:

1. Develop a professional operation capable of dealing with the complex and growing volume of the work.
2. Provide good value for money commensurate with the required level of customer service.
3. Sustain growth in a robust manner.
4. Meet the continuing renewal requirements of Motability's existing customers.
5. Plan for the future funding of those users needing more financial assistance because of increased disability.
6. Continue to improve and broaden the services provided by Motability in assisting disabled people with their mobility problems.

The measures being taken to meet these strategic aims have been described in earlier chapters. Above all, Motability will use its very considerable and increasing purchasing power to bear down on costs, passing on the benefits to its customers. An example of this is the reduction of leasing costs made

148

possible by the negotiation of a new insurance contract with Royal & Sun Alliance, and the proposals for changes in car maintenance and residual values described earlier. The motor industry and the manufacturers of adaptations and special vehicles will also be encouraged to show increased flexibility in meeting the needs of disabled people.

As an example of the broadening of its work in the future, Motability is seeking to establish with the Research Institute for Consumer Affairs an impartial advice service to assist disabled people in the choice of their vehicle. It may be possible to offer this and other advice and facilities to disabled drivers and passengers not using Motability's car schemes e.g. by enabling them to benefit from the preferential rates of insurance available to the main body of customers. Some of these people, although severely disabled, may not be eligible for the qualifying allowance – their disability may take the form of severe upper limb deformities, or they may be too old to qualify.

THE WAY AHEAD

In the years since it first offered its services in 1978, Motability, although by no means complacent, can fairly claim to have been successful in its aim of providing personal mobility on affordable terms to very large numbers of disabled people, and of bringing about a transformation in their daily living.

It is often overlooked that the provision of personal transport through Motability brings many benefits to the community and to the Health and Social Services, as well as to the individual disabled person. For example, people with Motability Scheme cars no longer need others to transport them for visits to the doctor, hospital appointments and treatment, outings to clubs, shopping, attendance at school and college and travel to work. As a result, there are appreciable savings in public expenditure and in the load carried by voluntary organisations, carers, friends and relatives. In this way Motability will continue to make a substantial contribution to the welfare of the community.

After 20 years of service, Motability approaches the Millennium with confidence. Through a continuation of the fruitful partnership which has been built up with the Department of Social Security, the clearing banks and MFL, motor manufacturers and dealers, insurance companies, roadside assistance companies, the mobility centres and the suppliers of adaptations and special vehicles, Motability's benefactors and the motoring organisations, it aims to improve its schemes and to make them even more widely known. In this way it hopes that an increasing number of disabled people will find it worthwhile to take advantage of what it seeks to provide – a better deal in the acquisition of a car than can be obtained anywhere else by people of limited means. Motability is ever conscious of the fact that the great majority of its customers have no alternative to using its services if they wish to acquire a car, since they do not have the credit rating to go elsewhere. It is therefore of great importance that Motability should strive continuously to improve the terms on which cars are made available to disabled people.

A FORWARD VIEW BY THE VICE CHAIRMAN OF MOTABILITY

This chapter concludes with a personal look into the future by the Vice-Chairman of Motability, Gerry Acher.

What a long way Motability has come since the germ of the idea – using innovative tax-based financing to provide family saloon cars to take the place of the old grey trikes. And what new vistas this has opened up for so many disabled people and their families. I think very few of those involved in Motability at the outset could have envisaged that we would have helped probably in excess of half a million families in our short period of operation.

We have successfully made the transition from being merely a conduit by which manufacturers of motor vehicles and powered wheelchairs/scooters could get their product to disabled people to moving towards a people-centred operation.

We are not there yet and indeed we have a long way to go, but our progress fills me with encouragement. Our path over the last few years has not been easy. We have had our growing pains – like any organisation growing at nearly 20% each year; in fact doubling our size every four years. But we have come out stronger, fitter and full of confidence.

Now we are set fair; the sails are trimmed, what of the future? We must continue towards becoming an organisation that is properly people focused. We have made massive strides in our customer care and understanding our customer needs but we still have a long way to go. At present about a quarter of those receiving the higher rate DLA have a Motability Scheme car. Why is it 25%? Should it be more, in other words are we actually meeting our customers' and potential customers' needs? Indeed should it be less? Is the solution we are providing really the right solution or would some other means of transport or some other financing package be better? The answer to all these questions lies in the minds of the disabled people claiming the higher rate DLA and with their families. We need to do much more work in understanding these people's viewpoints, their aspirations and their fears. That we shall progressively do over the coming years.

But is the present solution the right solution? We know our leases have to be more flexible and we are working hard revisiting this whole area. Many people would like to have a longer lease than a three year lease and others would like to buy their cars at the end of their lease. We must certainly, over the coming years, be able to cater for a broader spectrum than we do at present.

Our growth has recently dropped to single digit figures; why? That we could not see this a year out is evidence that we need to understand our market place better. People are still apprehensive at sharing their concerns with us for fear of rocking the boat and losing their car or not having their lease renewed. This fear culture becomes more marked at times as at present with the Government's Benefit Integrity Project now really under way. *'Will I be next?'* *'Should I hold on to my old jalopy, dangerous as it is – at least no-one can take this away from me?'*

151

These are just some of the communication areas we have to work hard on over the next few years. Fear particularly when combined with loneliness is a terrible thing; our customers must look to us for support as the caring charity that we are.

We must continue to provide best value for money to our customers and use our significant buying power as effectively as possible. Six per cent of the new car registrations in the UK enables us to get the best deals and these we must get from all our service providers right across the board. But value for money is not just a monetary expression; there must be service as well. Our customers need a special type of service. We cannot just hand our customers the keys to their cars and expect them to need no support during the three year period of the lease. It is the balance that is so necessary and so important. It is this extra service that makes all the difference whether it is a courtesy car, while our customer's car is being serviced, or preferential treatment after an accident or at the side of the motorway in the event that a car breaks down. That is what Motability stands for.

And what about the more severely disabled person? The Government takes the responsibility for these people's mobility needs through the Mobility Equipment and Drivers Fund. There is a long long way to go before we have the right approach here. The monies involved are large and the solutions complex. When the solutions work, the freedom given to our customers is immense. In the rare times that the solutions do not work, this is a massive waste of effort and money. We look forward to working with Government to find the proper answer for the more severely disabled person who needs to drive from his or her own wheelchair.

As we move into an era where the name of the game is conservation of resources we at Motability must play our full part in making sure that our solutions are not just the most cost effective but the most environmentally, ecologically and socially acceptable. The more that can be designed into cars, when they are built, that meets the needs of the disabled person and the less mobile older person the better will be the solution. So much can be done at the design stage and it is in

152

this area that Motability really has something to offer. I look forward to real progress in the coming decade. Better car design makes for more satisfied customers, better solutions and real cost effectiveness. But we have a long way to go competing against all the other demands on the motor industry. Soon we shall also have to consider whether a three-year lease is the right basic product and the best use of resource. The economics are the most effective but if we were to leave our cars with our customers for longer, and were able to recycle safely significantly adapted vehicles, there will be strong advantages.

These are just a few of the challenges that we face over the next ten years but we cannot overcome them alone. This can only be done with the help of Government, of the disabled people's organisations, the manufacturers and the other service providers and of course our partners, MFL and the banks. The support we have received from all of these and from the first class team of committed people at Harlow fills me with confidence that Motability is really fit for the future.

Motability's Governors and in particular its Chairman, Lord Sterling, with his boundless energy and wise counsel will ensure that disabled customers' best interests are always kept in the full frame. It is a great sadness that our founder, Lord Goodman, is not with us to be able to reflect on the achievements of the first 21 years. We know that Motability was the most important thing that he ever started. I know that he would have been proud to have shared our strategy for the future. But I am proud that so many of those involved with Motability in 1977, like Allan Beard whose steady hand and strong support as Treasurer and friend has been so important to me as Vice-Chairman, are still on the Governing Board today. Our future strategy can only be the right strategy if it fits easily with their own aspirations for Motability and I am pleased to say it does.

153

APPENDIX 1

Vehicles Supplied

	Contract hire	HP new	HP used	Total cars	Wheel-chairs	Total vehicles
1978–82	12,404	5,895	874	19,173	833	20,006
1983	3,915	4,656	1,141	9,712	858	10,570
1984	4,217	5,058	1,354	10,629	821	11,450
1985	5,436	5,509	1,461	12,406	820	13,226
1986	11,693	5,953	1,183	18,829	712	19,541
1987	17,530	5,885	853	24,268	655	24,923
1988	21,357	7,064	646	29,067	807	29,874
1989	31,808	4,692	587	37,087	926	38,013
1990	40,299	2,873	685	43,857	900	44,757
1991	44,136	2,324	1,145	47,605	1,005	48,610
1992	57,898	2,896	1,587	62,381	1,364	63,745
1993	69,748	4,542	2,949	77,239	1,924	79,163
1994	82,471	4,674	2,980	90,125	2,273	92,398
1995	98,268	4,314	2,443	105,025	2,260	107,285
1996	119,071	4,090	2,365	125,526	2,012	127,538
1997	132,266	2,713	2,530	137,509	2,092	139,601
TOTALS	752,517	73,138	24,783	850,438	20,262	870,700

APPENDIX 2

Mobility Allowance Recipients and Motability Scheme Customers

At end of	Recipients of mobility allowance*	People with current agreements for Motability Scheme cars	Percentage of recipients with Motability Scheme cars
1982	248,860	14,744	5.9
1983	297,069	19,672	6.6
1984	363,605	26,152	7.2
1985	428,177	32,365	7.6
1986	485,661	41,256	8.5
1987	539,602	53,786	10.0
1988	587,190	68,714	11.7
1989	633,451	85,657	13.5
1990	678,119	103,478	15.3
1991	717,913	121,761	17.0
1992	844,607	145,571	17.2
1993	956,461	178,317	18.6
1994	1,032,121	212,566	20.5
1995	1,138,566	225,876	19.8
1996	1,248,600	302,594	24.2
1997	1,538,800	345,525	22.4

* Or the higher rate mobility component of the disability living allowance. Includes war pensioners' mobility supplement cases.

APPENDIX 3

Grants from Motability's charitable fund

Year ending 31 March	£
1979	41,695
1980	150,464
1981	103,968
1982	79,743
1983	139,151
1984	97,995
1985	154,583
1986	249,717
1987	189,411
1988	204,248
1989	366,059
1990	497,663
1991	1,281,334
1992	2,493,748
1993	2,928,300
1994	2,363,311
1995	2,132,115
1996	2,275,742
1997	1,623,144
1998	2,958,311

APPENDIX 4

Principal Supporters of Motability

Automobile Association
Bernard Sunley Charitable Foundation
British Petroleum
CHK Charities
Eagle Star
Enkalon Foundation
Esmee Fairbairn Charitable Trust
Esso Petroleum
Fiat
Fleet News
Ford
General Electric
Glaxo Wellcome
Henry Smith Estates Charities
Honda
Ladbroke Group
LASMO
Lazard Brothers and Co
Lloyd's Charities Trust
London Law Trust
Marks and Spencer
Mercury Communications
Morgan Grenfell Group
Mrs P.J. Sheridan Charitable Trust
NFC Foundation
Nuffield Foundation
Panmure Gordon and Co
Peninsular and Oriental Steam Navigation Co
Renault

Rollins Hudig Hall Insurance Services
Rolls-Royce
Rover
Royal Automobile Club
Royal & Sun Alliance
Shell UK
Sir Jules Thorn Charitable Trust
Skoda
Tesco
The Adint Foundation
The Alan Edward Higgs Charity
The Alchemy Foundation
The Allied Dunbar Staff Charity Fund
The Astor Foundation
The Baring Foundation
The Bruce Wake Charity
The Childwick Trust
The Christopher H.R. Reeves Charitable Trust
The Clore Foundation
The Clothworkers' Foundation
The Cooper Charitable Trust
The Cotton Trust
The Gannochy Trust
The George Wimpey Charitable Trust
The Gilbert Edgar Trust
The Harold Hyam Wingate Foundation
The Hayward Foundation
The Hull & East Riding Charitable Trust
The John and Lucille van Geest Foundation
The John Ellerman Foundation
The Kirkby Laing Foundation
The Lady Hind Trust
The Late Barbara May Paul Charitable Trust
The Lord Cozens-Hardy Trust
The MacRobert Trusts
The Mercers' Charitable Foundation
The National Power Charitable Trust
The Notgrove Trust

The P.F. Charitable Trust
The Rank Foundation
The Rayne Foundation
The Robertson Trust
The Rose Flatau Charitable Trust
The Schroder Charity Trust
The Simon Gibson Charitable Trust
The Sir James Knott 1990 Trust
The Sobell Foundation
The Steel Charitable Trust
The Sue Hammerson Foundation
The Talbot Trusts
The Tudor Trust
The W.O. Street Charitable Foundation
The Weinstock Fund
The Welton Foundation
The Wolfson Foundation
The Zochonis Charitable Trust
Unilever
Vauxhall
Vickers

APPENDIX 5

Mobility Centres

Centres accredited by the Forum of Mobility Centres

Banstead Mobility Centre
Damson Way
Fountain Drive
Carshalton, Surrey SM5 4NR
Telephone 0181-770 1151

Cornwall Friends Mobility Centre
Tehidy House
Treliske Hospital
Truro, Cornwall TR1 3LJ
Telephone 01872 54920

Derby Regional Mobility Centre
Kingsway Hospital
Kingsway
Derby DE3 3LZ
Telephone 01332 371929

Disability Action
2 Annadale Avenue
Belfast, Northern Ireland
BT7 3UR
Telephone 01232 491011

Edinburgh Driving Assessment Centre
Astley Ainslie Hospital
133 Grange Loan
Edinburgh EH9 2HL
Telephone 0131 537 9192

Kilverstone Mobility Centre
2 Napier Place
Thetford, Norfolk IP24 3RL
Telephone 01842 753029

Mobility Advice and Vehicle Information Service (MAVIS)
'O' Wing
Macadam Avenue
Old Wokingham Road
Crowthorne, Berkshire RG45 6XD
Telephone 01344 661000

Mobility Centre
Hunters Moor Regional Rehabilitation Centre
Hunters Road
Newcastle-upon-Tyne NE2 4NR
Telephone 0191 219 5694

Mobility Information Service
Unit 2A
Atcham Estate
Shrewsbury, Shropshire SY4 4UG
Telephone 01743 761889

Wrightington Mobility Centre
Wrightington Hospital
Hall Lane
Wrightington
Wigan, Lancashire WN6 9EP
Telephone 01257 256280

Associate Members of the Forum

The Driving Assessment Service
Hillcrest
Moseley Hall Hospital
Alcester Road
Birmingham B13 8JL
Telephone 0121 442 3434

Irish Wheelchair Association
Blackheath Drive
Clontarf
Dublin 3
Ireland
Telephone 00 3531 8338241

Oxford Driving Assessment Centre
Mary Marlborough Centre
Windmill Road
Headington
Oxford OX3 7LD
Telephone 01865 227577

Officers of the Forum of Mobility Centres

Chairman
Morigue Cornwell MBE (Banstead Mobility Centre)

Secretary
Barbara Hatton (Wrightington Mobility Centre)

Treasurer
Anne Gray (MAVIS)

163

APPENDIX 6

Examples of Grants

Some examples of grants are given below. The prices of cars and adaptations are regularly increased, and grants for the purposes of these cases would undoubtedly now be higher than when these cases were selected. It should be made clear that in each case the applicant committed the higher rate mobility component of his or her disability living allowance (plus in many cases a lump sum contribution of £500 or £250) towards the leasing or purchase of the vehicle; the grants made were to bridge the gap between the finance produced by the mobility component, plus any contribution from the applicant, and the total cost of the transaction.

From Motability's charitable fund

Mr A, aged 66 and weighing 15 stones, had severe arthritis in his spine, which affected his walking ability, and in his arms, which prevented him from propelling himself in his manual wheelchair.

Mr A's mobility was therefore severely restricted, and he was dependent upon his 65-year-old wife to push his wheelchair and to load it into their car. She was finding this increasingly difficult, so that Mr A had become almost housebound. When it was essential that they went out, he would drive and wait in the car while she did the shopping.

The couple depended entirely on Social Security benefits and had no savings. Motability encouraged him to seek full mobility and advised his health visitor about organisations which could help with the funding of an electric wheelchair. As a result, the British Legion provided an electric scooter.

Motability's part in this operation was to make a grant of £2,953 to cover the initial rental on a new Vauxhall Astra estate car with automatic transmission, power-assisted steering and ramps at the rear, so that the scooter could be loaded easily and without strain.

Mr B, aged 39, had multiple sclerosis, giving him an unsteady gait and weakness in both legs and in his right arm and hand. He was married, with four children aged from nine months to ten years. The household income came entirely from Social Security benefits.

Mr B had applied for a grant to enable him to obtain a large automatic estate car. There would, however, have been insufficient seats for all the children in this car. Motability therefore gave a grant of £5,326 for the initial rental of a Renault Espace with automatic transmission and power steering. This enabled Mr B to take his whole family out together, with the children suitably seated and restrained.

Master C, aged ten, was seriously ill, had been born with a defective liver and undergone an unsuccessful transplant, and was waiting for another. He lived with his parents and three brothers and sisters. The family income came solely from Social Security benefits, and there were no savings.

A car was needed to enable them to travel together as a family. Motability gave a grant of £2,139 for the initial rental of a Nissan Serena, which had enough seats for them all to travel in safety and comfort.

Mrs D was only 33, but had rheumatoid arthritis and suffered from the results of a stroke. She lived with her husband, who was her full-time carer, and their four children, aged between 11 and four years. Their only income was from Social Security benefits.

Mrs D was a wheelchair user, but did not wish to travel in the chair in a car, preferring to sit in the front with the family. A vehicle was needed that would enable her husband to lift her easily into the passenger seat and would accommodate the entire family and Mrs D's electric wheelchair.

165

The Nissan Serena, with its large side door and ample seating, was identified as the most suitable vehicle for Mrs D's needs, and accordingly a grant of £2,139 was given for the initial rental.

Mrs E was aged 45, and had suffered injuries to her left leg in a road traffic accident some eight years previously. Some of these injuries had not healed properly, and this, coupled with arthritis in her right side, severely restricted her mobility. She had not driven since her accident, but wished to resume driving. Her only income was from Social Security benefits.

Motability felt that specialist advice should be sought, and paid for Mrs E to have an assessment at an assessment centre. The centre recommended a number of adaptations to enable Mrs E to drive comfortably, and it was found that these were available as standard on the Renault Clio automatic with power steering. A grant of £1,276 was given towards the initial rental of this vehicle and a hoist to enable Mrs E to load her wheelchair into the boot.

From the Mobility Equipment Fund

Mr F, aged 33, suffered from cerebral palsy, hydrocephalus and scoliosis, and weighed 16 stone. He lived with his parents, his sister and her two young children, and the household was receiving Social Security benefits. There were no savings.

Mr F was confined to a wheelchair and could no longer sit in the family Vauxhall Astra without injury to his health. In any case, because of his weight his relatives were unable to lift him in and out of a car. The Nuffield Orthopaedic Centre were prepared to supply a custom-moulded system to fix to his wheelchair if a suitable road vehicle could be provided through Motability.

Mr F normally attended a day centre, but because of the lack of suitable transport he had been unable to do so for the last year.

A vehicle was required which Mr F could enter from the rear in his powered wheelchair by means of ramps, and with suffi-

166

cient room for the equipment which he had to carry with him. A Nissan Versa was demonstrated and found suitable. His sister was to be the driver, and as she suffered from osteo-arthritis she needed the power-assisted steering which was standard on the Versa, plus a Guido Simplex clutch for ease of gear changing.

A grant of £8,420 was made towards the cost of a five-year contract hire agreement for the vehicle.

Miss G, aged 23, suffered from spina bifida and hydrocephalus, being totally paralysed below the waist. She lived with her parents and was employed as an office clerk, with wages of £56 a week. She had savings of £675.

She was coming to the end of a contract hire agreement through the Motability Scheme for a Ford Escort, made with the aid of a previous grant. The mileage on this car was only 3,800, apparently because Miss G had found it difficult to drive – she said that the engine was too powerful and the car too large.

A grant of £2,672 was made towards the cost of a Renault Clio on contract hire, with adaptations including the removal and modification of the Car Chair system previously fitted to the Escort. The grant was after the normal contribution of £250 from Miss G, but no account was taken of her savings.

Mrs H, aged 34, suffered from progressive multiple sclerosis, and was confined to a wheelchair. She lived with her elderly parents, both pensioners, and her son, aged nine. She was receiving Social Security benefits and had no savings. The parents were the drivers of her car, a Ford Fiesta, which was coming to the end of a contract hire agreement.

It was clear that for the next lease a rear-access vehicle would be needed. A Fiat Fiorino was demonstrated and found to be ideal, with the addition of a winch to pull Mrs H's wheelchair up the ramps in the rear and an additional seat for the child. A grant of £4,500 was made for the cost of a five-year contract hire agreement for the Fiorino, fitted with the winch and seat.

In view of Mrs H's financial circumstances, the normal contribution of £250 was waived.

Master J, aged 12, was disabled with cerebral palsy and was confined to an electric wheelchair. He weighed seven stone. He lived with his mother and four other children, one over 16. His mother had some part-time earnings and Social Security benefits.

The lease of the existing Motability Scheme car, a Ford Escort, was close to expiry. Because of her son's increasing weight and back problems Mrs J was finding it very hard to manoeuvre her son in and out of the Escort and to stow his wheelchair in the car, and a different vehicle was clearly required.

After a demonstration, a grant of £5,604 was made towards the three-year contract hire of a rear-access vehicle, a Renault Versa. It was suggested to Mrs J that she should consider buying the Versa at the end of the lease under Motability's used car scheme.

From the Drivers Fund

Mr K, aged 23, suffered from congenital spinal lesions, causing restricted movement and strength in all four limbs, and was confined to a powered wheelchair. He held a provisional driving licence and wanted a car which he could drive from his chair. Mr K was a student, living alone and entirely dependent on Social Security benefits, with no savings.

After an assessment at MAVIS it was decided that a Ford Transit was required, with extensive modifications. These included joystick steering and wheelchair tie-down.

There could be no guarantee of repurchase by the dealer at the end of a lease on such a heavily-adapted vehicle, and it therefore had to be supplied on hire purchase. This was in any case advantageous both to Motability and the applicant, because it eventually became his property.

The total cost of the vehicle and adaptations was £29,291. Only £80 per four weeks of the mobility component was asked for from Mr K, leaving him with a substantial part of the allowance for insurance and maintenance. A grant was made of £25,013.

APPENDIX 7

The Motability Customer Charter

Applications

All correctly completed application forms will be actioned within two working days of receipt.

All authorised applications will result in Motability producing agreements for despatch to the customer's chosen supplier within three working days of receipt.

Agreements for first-time applicants and hire purchase customers will be sent to the chosen supplier by first-class mail.

All other agreements will be sent by second-class mail.

Letters

All written correspondence will be responded to within four working days.

All customer grievances/comments will be responded to within four working days.

Wherever possible, Motability will attempt to provide the customer with a constant point of contact within the Customer Information Services and Terminations Departments.

Telephone calls

All calls will be handled with understanding.

The average call response rate for customers' calls will be no longer than 30 seconds.

Motability is organised to ensure continuity of customer contact. Wherever possible, the customer will be assisted by one member of staff for any specific enquiry, although this is not always possible on the busy telephone services. The customer will be advised of the name and direct line contact number of the member of staff dealing with the enquiry.

Contract renewal

All customers who have an existing agreement and the necessary award qualification will receive a renewal invitation up to six months in advance of the expiry of their current agreement.

All renewal applications submitted in good time which meet the necessary criteria will result in Motability's producing agreements for despatch to the supplier and will enable the customer to benefit from up to three months' advance payment price protection.

Grant applications

Receipt of the application form for financial help will be acknowledged within two days.

Financial help will be considered towards the least expensive suitable solution to meet each applicant's basic mobility needs.

A letter of confirmation as to whether or not the applicant is accepted onto the waiting lists will be sent within ten working days.

Updates will be given in writing at regular intervals.

Priority will be given to renewal customers. Every effort will be made to ensure continuous mobility, provided that the completed renewal request is returned in good time.

The Grants Department operates an appeals procedure, written details of which are available on request.

Any vehicle that is supplied with significant modification will be inspected before delivery.

As part of Motability's continuous improvement programme, a customer satisfaction enquiry is being made following vehicle delivery in every grants case.

Contract termination

Motability will action all requests to terminate contracts within three working days of receipt.

In the case of early terminations, wherever possible a decision to decline assistance with termination costs or proceed towards a charitable grant offer will be notified to the customer within ten working days. (This does not apply to Mobility Equipment Fund or Drivers Fund cases, where the Governors on the Grants Committee have to approve the decision.)

APPENDIX 8

The First Class Suppliers Charter

ACCREDITATION OF SUPPLIERS

To qualify as a First Class Supplier, a dealer who supplies new cars will be subject to regular inspection on site so that Motability can be assured that they are ready and able to provide customers with a first-class service. The standards to be met are set by Motability and are under constant review. Reaching these standards is essential for every supplier who wants to become Motability Accredited. Suppliers who do not meet the standards will no longer be able to carry out business on the Motability contract hire scheme.

The performance of First Class Suppliers is monitored by Motability through on-site inspections, customer surveys, customer telephone calls and written correspondence.

MANDATORY STANDARDS FOR FIRST CLASS SUPPLIERS

The following standards are mandatory for Motability Accreditation:

On-site requirements

Toilets for disabled people in line with forthcoming legislation. Suitable parking spaces for disabled people.

Access for disabled people and wheelchairs to service and sales areas.
Suitable arrangements for customers who use wheelchairs.
Clear signs to all departments.
An accessible waiting area for customers.
Clearly displayed hours of opening.
A supply of Motability application brochures for customers to apply to the Scheme.

Services to be available

Refreshment facilities.
Use of a telephone, as appropriate.
The offer of a test drive/ride before application.
Core models in the small/medium car range to be available for demonstration.
Use of a Motability agreed handover and handback procedure.
Implementation of Motability agreed standards for inspection and reporting.
A documented customer complaints procedure.
Priority to be given to disabled customers, taking into account their disability and mobility needs, who have broken down or need urgent mechanical repairs.

Staff requirements

Minimum of one member of staff with knowledge of basic vehicle adaptations, local agents and mobility centres.
Motability specialists to have a copy of and understand the Fair Wear and Tear Guide.
Staff to hold a current Motability Accredited certificate (on completion of an Accredited training course).
A minimum of 90 per cent correct completion of paper work to be sent to Motability/Motability Finance Limited.
A deputy to be in place to give Motability Accredited advice during holidays or sick periods.

DESIRABLE STANDARDS FOR FIRST CLASS SUPPLIERS

On-site

Copies of Motability's magazine *Lifestyle* to be available for customer use.
Manufacturers' price lists to be available for customer use.

Services

Standard model courtesy car facilities.
Customer and vehicle collection and drop-off facility.
Automatic transmission models to be considered when selecting demonstrators for Motability Scheme customers.

Staff

Additional sales staff trained to Accredited standards.
After-sales representative trained to Accredited standards.

APPENDIX 9

Members of the Technical Development Committee and the Technical Advisory Group

Members who served on the Technical Development Committee at some time from 1988 to 1997
Adrian Stokes (Chairman)
David Alston (Motor manufacturers)
Gordon Bashford (British Leyland)
Dr George Cochrane (Mary Marlborough Lodge)
Morigue Cornwell (Queen Elizabeth's Foundation for the Disabled)
Capt. Brian Cross
Laura Ellis (MFL)
Dr Chris Evans (Royal Hospital and Home for Incurables)
Ann Frye (Department of Transport)
Robert Glossop (Queen Elizabeth's Foundation)
Geoffrey Goodman
Peter Harms (Department of Health)
Derek Harris (Formerly of the Oxford Orthopaedic Engineering Centre)
William Logan (Mitsui-Rikadenshi Ltd)
Campbell McKee (Transport Mobility Products Association)
John McNulty (Modular Technology Ltd)
Ann Mells (Mobility Advice and Information Service)
Ray Millichamp (Department of Health)
Fred Nailor (Disabled Drivers Association)
David Parkes (Department of Health)
Caroline Reed (Royal Association for Disability and Rehabilitation)
John Reynolds (MFL)

175

Tony Shipley (Department of Health)
Jill Vernon (Association for Spina Bifida and Hydrocephalus)
John Walker (Department of Health)
Bill Walmsley (Department of Health)
Neil Wood (University of Birmingham)

Secretary – John van Dongen

Members of the Technical Advisory Group
Mike Richards (Chairman and Motability's Grants and Technical Director)
David Alston (Motor manufacturers)
Morigue Cornwell (Queen Elizabeth Foundation)
Brian Dietz (MFL)
Ann Frye (Department of Transport)
Alan Lynch (Department of Health)
Campbell McKee (Transport Mobility Products Assn)
Edward Stait (MAVIS)
Adrian Stokes (Motability Governor)
Neil Wood (Birmingham University)
Jim Kerr (Motability's Technical Projects Controller)

APPENDIX 10

Surveys of Motability's Customers

Major surveys of Motability's customers were carried out in 1984 and 1993. The first was a general survey, covering the car hire and the car and wheelchair hire purchase schemes; the second was limited to users of Motability's main scheme, the car-hire scheme.

THE 1984 SURVEY

The survey was carried out among Motability's potential users, current users and past users. A total of 2,198 postal questionnaires was sent to these groups, among which the response rate varied from 70 to 86 per cent. The characteristics of the people responding corresponded closely with those in Departmental records.

The findings of the survey are best expressed in the form of answers to a series of questions:

What kinds of people could make use of Motability's services?

The people surveyed were those recently awarded the mobility allowance, but not using Motability. Nine out of ten were unemployed, and 60 per cent lived in one- or two-person households in which there was no one working. The most common self-reported descriptions of disability were arthritis, heart trouble, breathing difficulties, stroke and back trouble. Almost half were car owners, and about three-quarters had regular access to a car. Although the majority expressed themselves as very or fairly satisfied with their present transport arrangements, a limited follow-up investigation showed that some of these had unnecessarily accepted a low level of mobility.

Why did some mobility allowance recipients not use Motability's services?

Allowance recipients who had received an introductory leaflet about the Motability Schemes but had not responded to the invitation to ask for more information about Motability's services were surveyed. Their failure to do so no doubt reflected the level of satisfaction expressed about transport facilities, the large proportion above retirement age and the high incidence of circulatory and respiratory diseases leading to progressive ill-health. A small-scale follow-up telephone enquiry suggested that in some cases acceptance of the present situation was misplaced and that counselling might help.

There was a strong recurring emphasis on financial problems which deterred people from applying: finding the advance payment or cost of adaptations, and running costs. The question was raised whether the availability of help from Motability's charitable fund was always understood.

As regards wheelchairs, it was apparent that the financial arrangements of the Motability Scheme limited its appeal and that some people would have benefited from advice about the right kind of chair.

Did Motability's publicity material give a clear enough picture of the services on offer?

The survey gave clear evidence that there was a need for improvement in Motability's introductory leaflet and in the detailed booklets covering its various schemes. Particular points which came out were the failure to appreciate that the schemes applied to passengers as well as to drivers, and to all kinds of people virtually unable to walk; the problem of short awards of mobility allowance; and the need for amplification of information about financial arrangements. Above all, there was a need for an improved marketing approach. The wheelchair booklet was also criticised.

How satisfied were users of Motability with the schemes and their vehicles, and how were those vehicles used?

Two-thirds of the car user sample were drivers, and the same proportion were female, 7 per cent were aged 16 or less, 5 per cent aged 17 to 21, and 19 per cent 22 to 44. 16 per cent were 65 or over.

Users (including those who had applied for financial help) generally gave favourable reactions, and there were few complaints about their dealings either with Motability or MFL. Those with cars were generally satisfied with them – 67 per cent were very satisfied. The size of vehicle was one area of complaint, either for reasons of access or because of difficulty in loading a wheelchair. Among the 24 per cent who had had adaptations fitted, one in ten were dissatisfied, usually, it appeared, because they had chosen inexpensive adaptations in order to minimize costs.

There was some discontent with the contact between dealers and Motability Scheme car users, and some people (although relatively few) found the servicing arrangements inconvenient. Motability Scheme car users were very dependent on their vehicles; 88 per cent used them on most days, and 45 per cent every day, the main uses being for shopping, social visits and medical treatment. The median weekly mileage was 100; over 90 per cent travelled at least 50 miles a week in their car. Four out of ten of those with a Motability Scheme car said they would be entirely housebound without it.

Owners of the two main powered wheelchairs were in general satisfied with them. 31 per cent, using various makes, said they would not repeat their choice if given a second chance – improved performance through more power and better kerb climbing were the main reasons given for wanting a better chair. Often this was because the chair had been chosen without adequate information. About two out of three powered wheelchair owners used their chairs on most days or

179

every day outdoors, but only 17 per cent used their chairs this frequently indoors. Although the main use was for shopping, often it was not essential to use the chair inside the shops. The size of the chair was the main drawback here, both for manoeuvrability and entry into shops. This item featured prominently in the points of dissatisfaction with the chair, but it did not seem to be a basis for changing it.

A key determinant of a wheelchair user's satisfaction with his or her present transport arrangements was access to a car as a passenger. Since car ownership or access to a car was low for wheelchair users, they tended to be less satisfied than some of the other samples in the survey.

Why did early terminations of car agreements occur, and how far were they due to weaknesses in the schemes?

A minority of early terminations were caused by ill-health or inability to continue to use the car. Where the car was found to be unsuitable the main factor was size, and it appeared that more initial guidance and financial help might reduce this problem.

Of those who terminated prematurely, 91 per cent were satisfied with the Motability Scheme, and 56 per cent with their car. Where there was a change of car, it usually appeared to be a reflection of the market – mobility allowance recipients, like any other group, would choose the best time for changing their car and, in the case of a hire purchase agreement, the most advantageous time for selling and buying, which might not always coincide with the normal period of their agreement. As compared with other sample groups, the early terminations group contained more people in the younger age groups, more who were employed and more who were buying their houses.

THE CAR HIRE CUSTOMER SURVEY 1993

Each month, renewal invitations are sent by Motability to customers whose agreements are due to expire within six months. Advantage was taken of this monthly mailing to send a questionnaire to 2,882 people whose hire agreements were due to expire in May 1993. Some 48 per cent of those receiving questionnaires responded.

The survey provided a valuable cross section of Motability's customers, as will be seen from the analysis below.

Age and disability

There were more men than women (60 per cent compared with 40 per cent). Over half were aged 41 to 64, and 28 per cent were over 65. The answers to a question about the main cause of disability covered a wide range of health problems, but some 61 per cent were in just five categories: arthritis (24 per cent), heart trouble (11 per cent), back trouble (10 per cent), breathing difficulties (9 per cent) and multiple sclerosis (7 per cent).

Employment

Only 9 per cent were in paid work, either full-time or part-time. 70 per cent classified themselves as permanently sick or disabled, a further 11 per cent were wholly retired from work, and 5 per cent were unemployed.

In only 28 per cent of households where the disabled person was not in paid employment was there someone else with a job contributing to the bills. This means that around two-thirds of all the households represented were without anyone in paid employment. Moreover, the vast majority of jobs held by other members of the household (between 80 and 90 per cent) were relatively low-earning: junior non-manual or service work (e.g. wages clerk, shop assistant); foreman, supervisor or skilled manual worker (foreman in timber yard, painter/decorator, technician); and semi- and unskilled manual work (cleaner, road sweeper, kitchen porter). At least 15 per cent of the jobs described were part-time only.

Country of residence

Nearly as many respondents lived in the North of England as in the South and Midlands taken together, and both Wales

181

and Scotland were represented. Only a small proportion lived in Northern Ireland.

Accommodation

A quarter of the respondents owned their accommodation outright, and a further third were buying theirs with the aid of a mortgage. Nearly 40 per cent lived in council property, with a further 5 per cent in the private rental sector. 43 per cent had a garage, and a further 6 per cent a car port. Around one-third had a parking space, and only 20 per cent were without any of these facilities.

Household composition

The majority of respondents lived in households with two adults. In 16 per cent there was only one adult, and in the remainder (23 per cent) there were three or more. These households were for the most part without children. Only 19 per cent had one or more children living at home.

COMPARISONS WITH THE 1984 SURVEY

Some comparisons are possible between this sample of car hire customers and the sample in the 1984 survey. The latter included customers of all car schemes and is therefore not directly comparable. In addition, differences may be accountable for in terms of differential non-response bias and/or real change in the profile of customers.

Overall, the later sample contained a rather higher proportion of women than the previous survey, and a higher percentage of people over 65. The car hire sample also shows a higher proportion of respondents living in the North of England compared with the South. This is almost exactly the reverse pattern to that found in the earlier survey.

Differences were also found in tenure of accommodation, with owner-occupiers comprising 58 per cent of the later survey and council tenants only 37 per cent. In the earlier survey, council tenants were in the majority (55 per cent), with owner-occupiers comprising only 38 per cent. Finally, garaging arrangements show an almost identical distribution for the two surveys, with around half in both claiming to have a garage or car port.

CHOICE OF CAR

Over 80 per cent of customers said that they were given their first choice of car. 12 per cent said they would have liked a bigger car. The single most important reason why people had not hired their first choice of car was that they could not afford the advance payment. A further 15 per cent of reasons related to dealers: either they did not stock the car wanted (10 per cent) or did not inform the customer of its availability (5 per cent).

More than a third of customers who were going to renew their car hire contract intended to stay with their current make of vehicle, and another third were likely to but wished to retain an open mind. However, 27 per cent were thinking seriously about changing or had definitely made up their minds to do so.

The main reasons given for wanting to change or thinking about changing included the need for a bigger car (19 per cent) or a car with a smaller advance payment. But a wide variety of other reasons were also given, ranging from the desire for an automatic car or one with power-assisted steering, to the need for a more economic model or one with more comfort or better access. Some customers had problems with their current make and did not want to repeat the experience, while others were dissatisfied with their current dealer and wanted to change. In a number of cases, customers simply wanted to try something different.

Comfort and access of chosen car

95 per cent of respondents said the comfort of the seat and amount of leg room in their cars was either 'very good' or

'fair'. In these respects, there was little difference between the main makes of car. Ease of access was described as 'very good' or 'fair' by 94 per cent of respondents. Customers with wheelchairs were less satisfied with the ease with which these could be stowed in their cars than with the aspects of comfort and access. 25 per cent said this was 'not very good' or 'not at all good'.

Adaptations to chosen car

28 per cent of customers had cars with automatic gears, 8 per cent with power-assisted steering, and 8 per cent with both. One or other of these features were especially common in Nissan cars, only 27 per cent of which were without either.

Some 86 per cent of cars were free of other adaptations or conversions. Those that had been installed mainly comprised wheelchair hoists, hand controls of various kinds, steering balls or spinners, pedal adjustments, switch adaptations and swivel seats.

Use made of cars

Three activities account for nearly two-thirds of the uses to which customers put their cars – shopping (22 per cent of uses mentioned), visiting family and friends (21 per cent) and attendance for medical treatment (20 per cent). Holidays and social outings were also important.

The average weekly mileage was 131, with a median of 120. Some 9 per cent of customers reported a weekly average which, over a year, would exceed the 12,000 miles allowed under the current leasing contract without further payment.

Person driving

In 26 per cent of cases the disabled person was the only driver, and in 23 per cent the driver was someone else. Half of the respondents said that who drove depended on circumstances. A higher percentage of customers over 65 said they were the only driver, but this was the main difference between the age groups. There were, however, marked differences between the sexes, with half as many women as men being the only driver, and three times as many always being driven by someone else.

EXPERIENCES WITH MOTABILITY

The proportions of customers who wanted improvements in various aspects of Motability's services were as follows:

	Per cent
Making application for a grant	35
Inquiries about changing to a different car	32
Advice about whether to hire or buy	28
Applying for a grant for conversions	21
Length of time the contract runs for	18
Advice on what to look for in a car	18
Advice on suitable conversions	18
Advice on choice of car available	17
Telephone enquiries	15
Pamphlets and printed information	12
Insurance cover	8

Some of the comments and suggestions under these headings are summarised below. Many of the points made have since been covered by the Motability Customer Charter.

Applications for grants

Many customers said that they did not know that grants were available. Other comments were about the difficulty in getting a grant, understanding the conditions, embarrassment about applying and the slowness of the operation. This last complaint is of course inevitable, given the need for a waiting list.

Changing to a different car

There were complaints about lack of information about the possibility of changing before the end of the hire period, delay in the process, and absence of sympathy from Motability where a change was necessary because of a deterioration in health.

Advice about whether to hire or buy

The main suggestion was that there should be better information. Some people said that they were not made aware that they could buy rather than hire.

Length of time a contract runs for

Some people would prefer a shorter hire period, but probably the majority would like it to be longer, largely for financial reasons i.e. to reduce the advance payment.

Advice on cars, adaptations and conversions

Some comments emphasised customers' concern that they were not given enough information to choose a car and/or adaptations meeting their individual needs, and that they were expected to specify what was required. Some customers would like to receive more detailed information on the makes and models of cars available under the hire scheme.

Telephone enquiries

Customers mentioned difficulties in making contact by telephone, the time taken for the telephone to be answered, delay in being put through to the correct person and dissatisfaction with replies.

Pamphlets and printed information

There were many suggestions for improvements. These concerned three main aspects: presentation, content and the general availability of information. Since the survey the main pamphlet about Motability cars has been redesigned and a periodical magazine, *Lifestyle*, has been introduced to provide information for customers, particularly on the matters mentioned above, on a more comprehensive basis and in a more informal way.

EXPERIENCES WITH DEALERS

Customers were asked about their experiences with the dealers who supplied their Motability Scheme cars. The proportions of customers who wanted improvements in various aspects of service were as follows:

	Per cent
Loan vehicle while car is at garage	45
Wheelchair-accessible toilets	28
Disabled parking convenient to reception	25
Wheelchair access to reception	20
Pick-up and return service not available	20
Waiting area not comfortable	16
Advice in choosing a vehicle unsatisfactory	13
Quality of overall service	13

Comments and suggestions made by customers under some of these headings are given below.

Loan vehicle while car is at garage

The main complaint was that the dealer did not supply a loan car while the customer's car was being repaired. Some people said that loan cars were not always well publicised and/or were offered grudgingly, that they were not always free of charge, that the car offered was not automatic, or that there was too long a waiting list.

Access

Some customers complained that toilets accessible to wheelchairs were not available or were unsuitable, that parking

187

convenient to reception was not available, and that wheelchair access to reception needed improvement.

Quality of overall service

Within the 13 per cent of customers who had complaints under this heading, many focused on what was said to be the 'uncooperative, unhelpful or rude' attitude of the garage. There were also complaints about the length of time to acquire spare parts or carry out repairs, and the cost and quality of the work done. Some people were convinced that they had been given 'rogue' cars.

EXPERIENCES WITH INSURANCE CLAIMS

Half of the respondents had not made any insurance claims during the contract period. 35 five per cent had made one such claim, 15 per cent two, and some 7 per cent three or more. Improvements were suggested in four aspects:

	Per cent
Promptness of initial inspection	12
Promptness with which repairs organised	11
Speed of completion of repairs	10
Quality of repair work	7

APPENDIX II

MOTABILITY'S
MANAGEMENT STRUCTURE

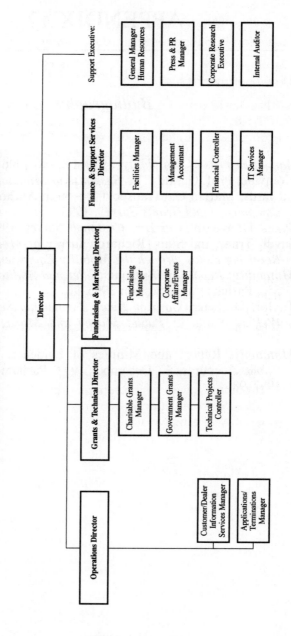

APPENDIX 12

Bibliography

Annual Reports of Motability, 1979–1980 to 1996–1997

Hoinville, Prof. Gerald, *The Response to Motability*, 1984

Edwards, Marian C. (Transport Research Authority), *Mobility Equipment Fund Grants Survey*, 1993

Sykes, Dr Wendy, *Car Hire Customer Survey*, 1993

Savill, Tracy and Stait, Richard, *Survey of Motability Clients Receiving Funds through the Mobility Equipment Fund*, 1995

Motability: Report by the Comptroller and Auditor General, HC 552, Parliamentary Session 1995–96

Taylor, Dr Peter, *Cash or Kind? Partnership Schemes and the Welfare State*, in *Public Money and Management*, March 1997

Motability, Report and Minutes of Evidence, Committee of Public Accounts, 17 December 1997, Parliamentary Session 1997–98